INSTANT POT MEDITERRANEAN DIET COOKBOOK FOR BEGINNERS

Mandy Cook

CONTENTS

INTRODUCTION

Today's home cooks have never been busier, struggling to balance their career and personal life. It is difficult to fit cooking into our busy schedules, right? I'm in the same boat. In the morning or after a long day at work, I often need a meal that I can put on the table in a hurry. I just want to throw my favorite ingredients into the pot and cook meal that doesn't require my full attention.

My desire to simplify my life and my love for cooking and Mediterranean sparked the idea for this recipe collection; my passion for Mediterranean foods led me to the Instant Pot, a programmable multicooker, which has experienced a renaissance in the 21st century. It allows me to make my favorite Mediterranean dishes year-round, whenever I'm on a jam-packed schedule but still crave something healthy and delicious. Who says a healthy breakfast casserole with fruits and grains has to bake for hours? According to this recipe collection, all you need is your Instant Pot and 20 minutes! Yes, the Instant Pot is a game changer! It can save your time by loading up the inner pot, choosing the right button and letting it do the rest. It can also save your money by cooking inexpensive cuts of meat, beans, and grains to absolute perfection. I also think that there is no better tool to show your dedication to healthy living and Mediterranean way of eating!

In developing this collection, I studied Mediterranean culinary classics and adapt them for use in the modern-day Instant Pot. I tried my best to design a healthy eating plan that includes authentic Mediterranean foods cooked in the Instant Pot. This eating plan focuses on high consumption of local, unprocessed foods, emphasizing whole grains, glistening fresh seafood, aromatic spices, and lots of fresh vegetables. On the other hand, it is characterized by low consumption of red meat, eggs, and dairy products. Processed and prepackaged foods are off limits here. Thus, healthy eating doesn't have to be time-consuming and boring – a diversity of the Mediterranean diet will amaze your family since it is endlessly adaptable with lots of fresh ingredients and immensely creative recipes.

Medical experts around the world have proven that the Mediterranean diet is one of the best dietary plans for modern humans. It is linked to many health benefits, including lower risk of cardiovascular disease, obesity, and diabetes. The Mediterranean diet reflects a fresh, sophisticated approach to the pressure cooking, requiring fresh ingredients and new flavor combinations, instead of the frozen vegetables and poultry you used to cook in your old pressure cooker. Are you ready to unlock the mysteries of successful pressure cooking and Mediterranean diet featured in this cookbook? Bon appétit! Buen provecho! Enjoy your meal!

THE BEGINNER'S GUIDE TO THE MEDITERRANEAN DIET

Did you know that one of the world's healthiest populations live in the Mediterranean region? Studies link their lowest rates of middle-age mortality to their eating habits. Food staples such as vegetables, fruits, and healthy fats keep them living long while moderate physical activity helps them stay vital in old age. The Mediterranean dietary regimen focuses on a good amount of fresh, seasonal vegetables and fruits, whole grains, and healthy nuts, as well as fish and shellfish.

When it comes to a healthy diet, my philosophy is pretty simple – a bowl of fresh vegetable sticks or a handful of raw nuts are my everyday snacks; my family eat fish or seafood two times per week; as for desserts, I like fresh or dried fruits since I want to give my body the best nutrients I can; however, having a dessert occasionally is an excellent way to relax and enjoy your life. There is one more simple rule – I try to eat fruits that grow close to my living place. This is the essence of the Mediterranean diet plan. As you probably already know, there is no one-size-fits-all diet plan so you should find a personalized nutrition plan that actually gives results. There are many versions of a Mediterranean diet plan. Some argue that red meat shouldn't be part of the Mediterranean diet, while others would say that dairy products are not healthy since they contain saturated fat. We could debate this subject forever, but many experts recommend the Mediterranean way of eating as a good option for improving your health and preventing serious diseases. How does it look in practice? I created the list of items that are essential for a Mediterranean pantry:

FRESH FRUITS – In fact, you should consume fresh fruits of all kinds. However, the key is to buy local and fresh products whenever possible. There is no need to buy expensive imported fruits. Some typical fruits that are most suitable for growing in the Mediterranean climate include citrus fruits (they grow in specific climates with warm summers and mild and moist winters, with lots of sunny days), pears, peaches, figs, apples, watermelon, cantaloupe, berries, and apricots. These fruits mostly need lots of sunshine and they are also sensitive towards low temperatures.

FRESH VEGETABLES – Obviously, consuming vegetables when they're in-season i.e. fresh from the farm, means they're fresher, healthier, and tastier. They include tomatoes, cucumber, eggplant, peppers, onions, okra, green beans, mushrooms, zucchini, peas, potatoes, cabbage, celery, broccoli, cauliflower, beets, carrot, lettuce, and leafy greens.

GREENS – Dandelion, amaranth, chicory, beet greens and leafy greens are essential for a healthy eating plan.

DRIED BEANS & LENTILS – An extremely important part of the Mediterranean diet is the consumption of beans and legumes. They're a good source of protein and dietary fiber for your body. They include beans, lentils, chickpeas, peanuts, and soy.

SEEDS – Seeds pack a nutritional punch that can provide physical and mental health benefits. In fact, no seeds are off limits on the Mediterranean diet. Pumpkin seeds, sunflower seeds, sesame seeds are all excellent sources of antioxidants, good fats, dietary fibers, and minerals.

NUTS – They are extremely nutritious; they may improve your health in many ways. Mediterranean nuts such as almonds, pistachios, cashews, hazelnuts, pine nuts, chestnuts are popular sources of omega-3 and omega-6 fatty acids as well as minerals and protein. Go nuts!

GRAINS – Bread (preferably whole grain bread), pita bread, oats, whole-grain pasta, rice (preferably brown rice), bulgur, buckwheat, barley, couscous, and polenta are the most commonly used grains on the Mediterranean diet. Whole grains contain a good amount of B vitamins, minerals such as magnesium zinc, and iron, dietary fiber, and antioxidants. Oats and buckwheat are nutrition superstars, loaded with complex carbs and many vitamins.

DAIRY PRODUCTS – In the traditional Mediterranean diet, people consume full-fat, plain dairy products such as Greek yogurt, mozzarella, parmesan, feta cheese, graviera, mitzithrao, sheep's milk yogurt and so forth.

EXTRA-VIRGIN OLIVE OIL – EVOO is an essential component of a healthy Mediterranean diet. It is called " liquid gold" because of its high amount of powerful antioxidants as well as healthy monosaturated fats. It has significant anti-inflammatory and anti-cancer properties too. You should buy olive oils in dark glass bottles or cans, since light can have a bad effect on the quality of extra-virgin olive oil. Keep your olive oil in a dark and dry place. Healthy fat sources on the Mediterranean diet include avocado, coconut oil, and avocado oil, too.

FISH & SEAFOOD – Whitefish, anchovies, sardines, shrimp and calamari deliver many important nutrients. Experts recommend eating one to two servings of seafood per week. Fish and seafood have been associated with a reduced risk of heart disease and stroke as well as depression and Alzheimer's Disease. Poached, baked and grilled fish are healthy choices; avoid fried fish and deep-fried breaded fish sticks or fillets.

CANNED TOMATOES – If you have a can of tomatoes in stock, you can stir up a quick Bolognese or any Mediterranean-inspired dipping sauce in no time. You can make a simple one-pot pasta recipe, you can jazz up your soup or use it in place of stock. The possibilities are endless! Homemade tomato ketchup comes together easily in the Instant Pot; simply cook a can of crushed tomatoes with onion, apple cider vinegar, brown sugar, and your favorite spices; afterwards, puree the ingredients with an immersion blender.

CONDIMENTS – Aioli, anchovy paste, honey, hot sauce, ketchup, mustard, salad dressings, tzatziki, and vinegar.

HOMEMADE BROTHS – A homemade bone broth or a long-cooked stock is a super versatile ingredient. As for Instant Pot and Mediterranean diet, it can be used in place of water if you want a deeper, richer taste of your meals. You can use bone broth, fish broth, or clam juice to add a rich twist to classic Mediterranean dishes. Moreover, add a splash of broth to deglaze the pan.

OLIVES – Who does not like mouthwatering Mediterranean olives on salads and sandwiches or alone with a glass of wine?! Besides being delicious, olives are a powerhouse of important vitamins such as Vitamin E, essential minerals, and antioxidants. They can control blood pressure and cholesterol, boost your immune system, and stimulate your digestive tract to work properly.

HERBS & SPICES – Parsley, oregano, basil, saffron, thyme, rosemary, sage, and cilantro are the most commonly used herbs on the Mediterranean diet plan. Other spices common to the Mediterranean Diet include mint, pul biber, lavender, marjoram, savory, sumac, anise, tarragon, bay leaf, chiles, cloves, cumin, and fennel seeds. High-quality seasonings can turn ordinary canned beans into a wholesome, delicious dinner for the whole family! Make sure to choose natural and organic ingredients without preservatives and colors. It is the secret to the best Italian, Spanish and Greek meals so spice it up!

Mediterranean diet promotes drinking of herbal teas such as chamomile, sage, mountain tea, thyme, parsley, and so on. Similar to berry juices and red wine, herbal teas contain polyphenols which are good for heart health.

BEVERAGES – Drinking more than eight glasses of water is beneficial for overall health. If you choose plain water over sodas and sugary drink, you will drastically reduce caloric intake. Drinking enough water can prevent dehydration, improve brain function, and control your energy level throughout the day.

This dietary regimen does encourage a moderate intake of fruit juices since it is centered around fresh fruits. However, you should choose homemade fruit juices as these tend to be lower in calories than store-bought products. The best options include apples and red berries (they contain polyphenols, too). A moderate intake of Greek yogurt, almond milk and Horchata (the Spanish tiger nut-based drink) is recommended on the Mediterranean diet. Red wine contains powerful antioxidants that play a significant role in preventing infections as well as serious diseases such as cancer and stroke. Raise a glass to your health!

To sum up, the Mediterranean diet emphasizes high intake of plant-based foods, moderate consumption of dairy products, seafood, poultry, and red wine, and low intake of red meat, eggs, and sweets. In order to balance the good with the bad, you can use red meat and eggs sparingly, since they are highly nutritious sources of protein and excellent sources of vitamin A and vitamin B-complex; in addition, you can replace a dark chocolate with unhealthy desserts. Foods that you should avoid at all costs include processed food, refined sugar, and highly refined oils. As for the Mediterranean way of eating, the golden rule says – cooking at home and keeping your pantry stocked with staple ingredients will help you stick to a healthy Mediterranean diet. Adopt these good habits and you can easily stop your cravings for sugar and other unhealthy items.

HOW TO ADOPT THE MEDITERRANEAN DIET FOR BETTER HEALTH?

Science has proven numerous benefits of the dietary patterns associated with the Mediterranean diet. In order to work properly, your body needs healthy and nutritious foods. The Mediterranean Diet is loaded with nutritious foods that improve your immune system, and hence the ability of your body to fight serious diseases. It actually promotes healthy eating habits, longevity, ideal body weight control, and good mental health.

Studies show that following a Mediterranean diet can improve your cognitive function (even 40 percent reduced risk for cognitive impairment). It also has positive effects on triglycerides and cholesterol as well as blood sugar (it can help you manage diabetes). Recent studies have shown that this dietary regimen may help to prevent osteoporosis and fight depression. The Mediterranean diet is rich in antioxidants so it can protect you against cancer and malignant diseases. Kale, red cabbage, berries, and beans are loaded with compounds that can protect your cells from free radicals; consequently, they increase your blood antioxidant levels to eliminate oxidative stress. Last but not least, the Mediterranean way of eating can help you lose weight and maintain your ideal weight in an easy and natural way. Improving your eating habits is not easy but it is achievable. First and foremost, you should consult your doctor before starting new diet. Here are a few tips that will help you lose pounds by following the Mediterranean lifestyle.

The non-diet approach. The Mediterranean diet is more than a dietary regimen, it is a lifestyle. The key to weight loss is making small lifestyle changes. Drinking enough water may help you lose weight in the long run. Prioritize good night's sleep, take vacations, and practice meditation to reduce stress and anxiety. Cooking at home may have a big impact on your overall health, weight, grocery budget, and relationships.

Opt for a wide variety of foods and go natural. Stock your kitchen with lots of natural, whole foods and you will avoid the temptation to eat unhealthy and processed foods. In other words, opt for real, unprocessed foods. You should base every meal around fresh fruit and veggies, seafood nuts, seeds, and herbs in their minimally-processed forms. Thus, minimize processed foods that are high in sugar, salt, and additives. Your body will thank you. Avoid unhealthy, simple carbohydrates which can be found in refined sugar, syrups, soft drinks and white flour. It is worth reiterating that you shouldn't go grocery shopping on an empty stomach.

Eat vegetables as a main course. Eat fresh, minimally processed vegetables as much as you can. Opt for steamed vegetables and start your meal with vegetable soup; low-calorie vegetables and soups can help fill you up so you will consume less high-calorie foods. If you like fried foods, cook your vegetables in a nonstick pan with a minimal amount of olive oil. Avoid breaded and deep-fried veggies.

Focus on good protein sources. You should consume fish and shellfish and plant-based protein. As for poultry, you should consume less than 3 ounces of chicken per week. Try to consume red meat such as beef and pork on rare occasions.

Aim for 25-30g of dietary fiber per day. Fiber can keep your digestive tract healthy and help suppress appetite. Increase fruit intake and limit the intake of sweets and processed foods. Only one small serving of pulses, three times a week, can improve your digestion and overall health.

Healthy fats. Good fats such as nuts, seeds, olive oil, and avocado are essential to our digestive system health and good metabolism. The human body needs fat to burn fat; thus, eating fat will not make you fat. It's a common misconception! The truth is, bad fats (like hydrogenated oils, artificial trans fats, and saturated fats) are linked to obesity, but good fats (unsaturated, poly and mono) are actually healthy. Additionally, if you do not consume enough fat, your body will not have enough energy to burn your body fat (in fact, it is stored, unnecessary energy).

Start exercising. If you are not particularly sporty, practice moderate and fun daily activities such as walking a dog, gardening or playing with children. Make sure to increase physical activity gradually to avoid possible negative outcomes. Get moving and find time to enjoy physical activity.

WHAT IS SO FASCINATING ABOUT AN INSTANT POT?

The Instant Pot is an electric multi-cooker designed to cook food under pressure at high temperature. It is intelligent, convenient, and programmable cooker that can speed up cooking process, save your money, and produce healthy food. It can do the job of nine different appliances – a regular cooking pot, pressure cooker, rice maker, steamer, slow cooker, warming pot, sauté pan, convection oven, and yogurt maker. Moreover, your intelligent multi-cooker has 14 cooking programs controlled by a built-in microprocessor inside the cooker; it actually controls main parameters such as the pressure, temperature, and time. You can simmer your soups and chowders, brown meat and fish, sweat vegetables or caramelize onions in your Instant Pot. You can make muffins and bread, prepare snacks, appetizers and even desserts.

Its innovative formula promotes global health and environmental sustainability, requiring minimal effort and cooking skills. How does it work? Your Instant Pot requires liquid such as water and broth; the liquid comes to a boil under an air-tight lid and it will turn into super-heated steam; consequently, the steam produces high temperature and pressure inside a cooking pot. Clever! In fact, you should put the ingredients into the cooking pot and seal the lid; then, choose the right button and Voila! Let the magic begin!

Manual – it is a "multi-purpose" button which allows you to adjust the temperature and time according to your recipe and personal preferences.

Slow Cook – thanks to this feature, you can use your Instant Pot as a conventional slow cooker, too. It is a great choice for busy weeknights and hectic mornings. Use this program if you like old-fashioned one pot meals.

Sauté – you can use this cooking program to sauté and sear your ingredients as well as to thicken the sauces and simmer the cooking liquid. Make sure to keep the lid open. Sautéing and browning are one of the best flavor-boosting techniques so you can maximize food's flavor with this option. If you are not in a hurry, sauté aromatics and sear meat before pressure cooking. This simple technique allows your food to bloom and release some of their hidden flavors. Do not clean your inner pot too early – use those caramelized bits from the bottom of the inner pot to enhance the flavor of your entire meal. Add a splash of dry wine, beer or broth for this purpose.

Meat/Stew – you can cook inexpensive, budget-friendly cuts of meat and old-fashioned stews just like grandma used to make. Use the "Adjust" button to change the cooking time and achieve the desired texture of your favorite meats. Adjust to "Less" mode if you like soft texture, "Normal" for very soft meat, and "More" for fall-off-the-bone meat.

Steam – this is an ideal program for quick-cooking items such as vegetables, fish, and seafood. Use 1 cup of water and steamer basket with this function.

Poultry – this program is for cooking the chicken to mouthwatering perfection since pressure cooking at high temperatures keeps the juices inside. If you like a golden, crispy top, simply turn the broiler on high and broil the chicken for a couple of minutes.

Rice – it is a fully automated program for cooking white rice or parboiled rice; it takes about 10 minutes to cook 2 cups of white rice. If you tend to cook brown rice or wild rice, simply use the "Manual" or "Multigrain" functions. Whit this smart cooking program, adapting your favorite Mediterranean rice recipes for the Instant Pot will be a breeze!

Multigrain – this fully automated program is perfect for making dishes with mung beans, brown rice, wild rice, farro, steel-cut oats, and cornmeal.

Bean/Chili – with this super useful program, you can cook your favorite beans from scratch. Say goodbye to canned beans!

Soup/Broth – you can make your own stocks and broths, hearty soups and chowders. Your cooker controls the pressure and temperature inside the cooking pot so you can achieve perfect results with minimal effort.

Porridge – the program is designed for all types of porridge such as congee and other grains. A quick tip: for the best results, always use a natural pressure release.

Yogurt – as the name indicates, you can make your own homemade yogurt.

Keep warm – Once the cooking cycle has completed, you can press the "Cancel" button, Otherwise, your Instant Pot will switch to the Keep Warm mode automatically; it will turn OFF after 10 hours.

The Instant Pot is an electric pressure cooker with two pressure release methods. The natural pressure release is perfect for porridge, congee, beans, and other starchy and foamy food. Let the pressure decrease on its own, slowly and gradually. It will take more than 10 minutes.

Another method is known as a quick pressure release. When the cooking cycle has completed, turn the handle to the "Venting" position and wait a minute or two for rapid release. This method is perfect for delicate veggies such as greens and cauliflower as well as fish and seafood with a fine and delicate texture. Finally, remove the cooker's lid when all pressure is released. You can use a cold kitchen towel to speed up the process.

From now on, you can cook up an entire Sunday supper in one pot, easily and effortlessly. The Instant Pot can be used to make one-pot meals, pasta, casseroles, entrées, and even bread and desserts. Most recipes in this collection require a few minutes of preparation time, while shorter cooking times are perfect for those situations when time is limited. Moreover, there is no risk of burning food in the Instant Pot, which makes it an ideal tool for busy weeknights. You can also rely on pantry staples such as stocks, sauce, and grains for faster results. Whole grains, legumes and vegetables are all well suited to use in the Instant Pot. And they are at the center of the Mediterranean diet. A well-balanced diet includes foods from the five major groups – fruits, vegetables, protein, grains, and dairy. It should fulfill all of your nutritional needs throughout the day.

TOP FIVE BENEFITS OF THE INSTANT POT

The best way to adopt healthy eating habits, lose weight, and improve your health is to start cooking at home. With the Instant Pot, making homemade meals on a daily basis becomes a breeze. There are numerous benefits of the Instant Pot. This amazing kitchen tool allows you to cook a wide range of dishes, from soups and sauces to fish and casseroles. Here are some of the key benefits of Instant Pot and pressure cooking.

Health benefits. Pressure cooked foods are healthy and nutritious. Vegetables are a powerhouse of valuable nutrients. Most vitamins are not quite heat-stable so long cooking time can destroy them. Steaming and blanching the vegetables by cooking them briefly in hot water or steam can help them to optimize nutrient retention. Most vegetables take 3 to 5 minutes to be cooked thoroughly. Pressure cooking can preserve nutrients better than any other cooking method. Moreover, pressure cooking preserves the natural color of your veggies so you will end up with visually attractive foods as well.

Feeding your body high-quality and nutrient-dense foods may help improve your immune system, heart health, and digestion; it may speed up your metabolism and lose weight, as well as maintain your ideal body weight. If you're overweight, you are at the high risk of numerous medical diseases and conditions. Compared to common cooking techniques such as simmering, frying or grilling, pressure cooking preserves up to sixty percent more nutrients! Moreover, your Instant Pot doesn't require additional oils and fats. These recipes focus on cutting out all the processed foods and consuming natural food prepared in your own kitchen. It will help you keep total calorie intake under control. What it all boils down to is that homemade meals that promote better health also promote weight loss.

Perfectly cooked meals. Forget on overcooked vegetables, burned dishes and tasteless, undercooked grains. Simply add the ingredients to the Instant Pot, press the right button and go about your business. You will return to a perfectly cooked meal! You do not have to stir your food or babysit your cooker since an intelligent microprocessor controls temperature, pressure and time.

You'll find more free time. Let's face it, if you work full-time, you probably struggle to make time to cook family dinner. The Instant Pot, a programmable pressure cooker, will allow you to cook multiple meals without monitoring them. Imagine all the possibilities – you can have an extra pot, rice cooker or the best nonstick skillet you can find! You can use 3-piece divided steamer baskets and cook your foods separately – fish, potatoes, corn, baby food, and much more at once. That's what I call INSTANT!

An ingenious way to save money. I like to use inexpensive foods and turn them into healthy and delicious family meals. Revive leftovers, bones and cheap, root vegetables, and create the best homemade meals ever!

Energy efficiency. The Instant Pot will cut cooking time by up to 70-percent. Unlike the heat on your stove top, the heat in an electric pressure cooker is persistent, which also boosts its energy efficiency. Go green!

INSTANT POT MEDITERRANEAN DIET RECIPES AND OUR RECIPE COLLECTION

When you tend to cook something special for your family and friends, this collection will be your go-to source for the best Instant Pot healthy recipes ever! This recipe collection covers the best recipes from countries that border the Mediterranean. This collection actually promotes both a simple and creative approach to the cooking, requiring healthy and sophisticated food combinations, instead of dumping meat, vegetables and dull spices into a cooking pot. Throughout this collection, you'll find 75 old-fashioned and innovative recipes, from easy family breakfast to delicious main dishes and delectable desserts. You will learn how to prepare them in an electric pressure cooker with confidence and ease.

These recipes can help you create the best, ethnic-inspired meals for you and your family and still spend less time in the kitchen. Moreover, you can plan your day since each and every recipe is accompanied by a suggested serving size, estimated cooking time, and nutrition analysis. Our collection is chock-full of delicious and fail-safe recipes, making dieting, shopping, and meal planning a cinch. You will also learn Instant Pot Do's and Don'ts that will help you improve your culinary skills. So, get ready and get to know the Mediterranean with your Instant Pot!

3-WEEK MEAL PLAN

This is a sample menu for three weeks on the Mediterranean diet.

DAY 1

Breakfast – The Ultimate Egg Salad

Lunch – Fava Bean Soup; Traditional Yellow Rice

Snack – 1 cup veggie sticks; 2 tablespoons hummus

Dinner – Easy Fish Goulash; lettuce salad

DAY 2

Breakfast – Perfect Morning Porridge

Lunch – Spicy Chunky Beef Soup; 1 serving of cabbage salad; 1 serving of cooked rice

Dessert – Orange and Almond Cupcakes

Dinner – Spanish Repollo Guisado; 1 ounce cream cheese

DAY 3

Breakfast – Eggs with Tomato and Ricotta Cheese; 1 slice of whole-wheat bread

Snack – 5-6 almonds; 1 peach (apple or pear)

Lunch – Spanish Stew with Green Beans; 1 serving of Easy Herb Artisan Bread

Dinner – All-Star Ziti Casserole

DAY 4

Breakfast – Old-Fashioned Sweet Bread; 1/2 cup Greek yogurt

Lunch – Rich French Soup; 1 sweet pepper; 1 slice of toasted bread

Dinner – Crunchy Couscous Salad

Dessert – Festive Orange Cheesecake

DAY 5

Breakfast – Almond Oatmeal Muffins

Lunch – Classic Minestrone with a Twist; 1 handful of mixed green salad with a few drizzles of a freshly squeezed lemon juice and extra-virgin olive oil

Dinner – Mediterranean Spicy Jambalaya

DAY 6

Breakfast – Oatmeal with Blueberries and Honey

Lunch – Ligurian Seafood Stew; 2 slices whole-wheat bread

Snack – 1 handful nuts and seeds

Dinner – Penne Pasta with Tomato Sauce and Mitzithra cheese

DAY 7

Breakfast – Giant Greek Tiganites

Lunch – Mom's Brussels Sprouts with Herbs; 1 cup of fried mushrooms with 1 tablespoon of olive oil

Dessert – Mixed Berry and Peach Compote

Dinner – Corn on the Cob with Feta and Herbs

DAY 8

Breakfast – Perfect Morning Porridge

Snack – 1 carrot, 1 celery stalk with 2 tablespoons of hummus; 1 apple

Lunch – Italian Red Lentil Soup

Dinner – Herby Juicy Chicken Fillets

DAY 9

Breakfast – Savory Mushroom Oatmeal

Lunch – Spanish Arroz Rojo with Beef

Dessert – Easy Blueberry Crumb Cake

Dinner – Steamed Artichokes with Aïoli Sauce; 1 serving of Easy Herb Artisan Bread

DAY 10

Breakfast – Fruit and Quinoa **Breakfast** Casserole

Snack – 1/2 cup of Greek yogurt; 1/2 cup of Mediterranean fruits

Lunch – Fisherman's Tilapia and Chickpea Stew; 1 serving of rice

Dinner – Layered Fish and Egg Salad

DAY 11

Breakfast – 1 cup yogurt with sliced fruits, seeds and nuts

Lunch – Rice with Red Sauce and Graviera Cheese; 1 tomato

Dessert – Apricot and Almond Crumble

Dinner – Shrimp Mélange with Bacon and Veggies

DAY 12

Breakfast – Old-Fashioned Greek Rizogalo

Lunch – Creamy Sopa de Zapallo; 1 serving of low-carb grilled vegetables

Dinner – Arroz con Pollo with a Twist

DAY 13

Breakfast – 1 pan-fried egg; 1 slice whole-wheat toast

Snack – 1 orange

Lunch – Italian-Style Aromatic Risotto; 1 grilled white fish fillet; 1 medium cucumber

Dinner – Mediterranean Chicken Bowl with Pine Nuts

DAY 14

Breakfast – 1 cup of Greek yogurt; 1/2 cup of fruits (apples or berries)

Lunch – Spanish-Style Quinoa with Pinto Beans; 1 handful of baby spinach with 1 teaspoon of mustard and 1 teaspoon of olive oil

Dessert – Brandy Chocolate Fudge with Almonds

Dinner – Red Skin Potato Mash with Pine Nuts

DAY 15

Breakfast – 2-egg omelet with onions and peppers; 1 ounce feta cheese

Lunch – Spring Wax Beans with New Potatoes; Sicilian-Style Brown Rice Salad

Dessert – Poached Apples with Greek Yogurt and Granola

Dinner – Sloppy Lentils in Pita

DAY 16

Breakfast – 1 ounce feta cheese; 1 bell pepper; 1 tomato; 1 serving of Banana Walnut Bread

Snack – Corn on the Cob with Feta and Herbs

Lunch – Traditional Greek Arakas Latheros

Dinner – Ultimate Vegetable Pot; 1 ounce feta cheese

DAY 17

Breakfast – Decadent Croissant Bread Pudding

Snack – 1 orange

Lunch – Grandma's Chicken Pilau; 1 serving of lettuce

Dinner – Yellow Cornmeal with Mediterranean Ragout

DAY 18

Breakfast – Omelet Mason Jars with Tuna

Snack – 1 orange; 1 apple

Lunch – Aromatic and Spicy Bulgur Wheat; 1 grilled white fish fillet:

Dinner – Mackerel Fillets with Authentic Skordalia Sauce

DAY 19

Breakfast – Orange and Almond Cupcakes; 1 apple

Lunch – Italian Cabbage with Portobello Mushrooms; 1 serving of cabbage slaw

Dessert – Jasmine Rice Pudding with Cranberries

Dinner – King Prawns in Tomato Curry Sauce

DAY 20

Breakfast – Easy Herb Artisan Bread; 1/2 cup Greek yogurt; 1 apple

Lunch –. Barbunya Pilaki (Turkish Bean Stew); 1 baked potato

Dinner – Italian-Style Eggplant and Chicken Casserole; 1 medium tomato with 2-3 Kalamata olives

DAY 21

Breakfast – Banana Walnut Bread; 1/2 cup of berries

Lunch – Old-Fashion Snow Pea Chowder; 1 pita bread; 1 serving of roasted cauliflower

Dinner – Creamiest Seafood Chowder Ever; 2 tablespoons tomato paste

Dessert – Festive Orange Cheesecake

BREAKFAST

1. The Ultimate Egg Salad

Servings 10

Ready in about
15 minutes

NUTRITIONAL
INFORMATION
(Per Serving)

150 Calories
11.6g Fat
2.6g Carbs
8.5g Protein
1.3g Sugars
0.7g Fiber

Ingredients

- 10 large-sized eggs
- 3/4 cup water
- Sea salt and freshly ground black pepper, to taste
- 1/4 teaspoon red pepper flakes
- 1/4 teaspoon saffron
- 1/4 teaspoon dill
- 2 tablespoons fresh parsley, chopped
- 4-5 radishes, thinly sliced
- A bunch of fresh scallions, chopped
- 1 cucumber, peeled and chopped
- 2 tablespoons ripe olive, pitted and chopped
- 1/2 teaspoon yellow mustard
- 1/4 cup mayonnaise
- 1/4 cup Greek yogurt

Directions

1. Put a metal rack inside your Instant Pot. Pour in 3/4 cup of water. Arrange the eggs on the rack.
2. Secure the lid and choose the "Manual" function; cook for 7 minutes at Low pressure. Once cooking is complete, use a natural pressure release; remove the lid carefully.
3. Immediately cool the eggs under cold running water; peel the eggs under water. Chop the eggs and transfer them to a nice salad bowl.
4. Fold in the rest of the above ingredients; gently stir until everything is well incorporated. Serve well chilled and enjoy!

2. Eggs with Tomato and Ricotta Cheese

Servings 3

Ready in about
15 minutes

NUTRITIONAL
INFORMATION
(Per Serving)

250 - Calories
18.6g - Fat
5.4g - Carbs
16.3g - Protein
2.3g - Sugars
0.9g - Fiber

Ingredients

- 1 tablespoon olive oil
- 1/2 purple onion, chopped
- 1 tomato, chopped
- 6 eggs
- 1/4 teaspoon red chili flakes
- 1/2 cup ricotta cheese, crumbled
- Sea salt, to taste
- 2 tablespoons fresh parsley leaves, roughly chopped

Directions

1. Press the "Sauté" button to preheat your Instant Pot. Heat the oil until sizzling; now, sauté the onion until tender and translucent.
2. Meanwhile, beat the eggs until the egg whites and yolks are well blended. Stir in the tomato, red chili flakes, and ricotta cheese.
3. Scramble the eggs in the Instant Pot using a wide spatula; cook and stir until everything is heated through. Sprinkle with sea salt.
4. Secure the lid. Choose the "Manual" mode and cook for 4 minutes under High pressure. Once cooking is complete, use a quick pressure release; carefully remove the lid.
5. Garnish with fresh parsley leaves and serve immediately. Bon appétit!

3. Almond Oatmeal Muffins

Servings 9

Ready in about 20 minutes

NUTRITIONAL INFORMATION (Per serving)

179 - Calories
9.3g - Fat
22.6g - Carbs
7.1g - Protein
8.5g - Sugars
3g - Fiber

Ingredients

- 2 tablespoons ghee, melted
- 1/4 cup honey
- 1/2 cup sour cream
- 1/3 cup full-fat Greek yogurt
- 3 eggs
- 1/3 cup plain flour
- 1 1/4 cups rolled oats
- 1/2 tablespoon baking powder
- 1/4 teaspoon ground cardamom
- 1/4 teaspoon ground star anise
- 1/2 teaspoon cinnamon
- A pinch of grated nutmeg
- A pinch of sea salt
- 1/2 teaspoon almond extract
- 1/2 teaspoon vanilla extract
- 1/2 cup almonds, chopped

Directions

1. Spritz a muffin tin with cooking spray.
2. Thoroughly combine the melted ghee, honey, sour cream, Greek yogurt, and eggs; mix until everything is well incorporated.
3. Now, fold in the plain flour, rolled oats, and baking powder; mix to combine; after that, mix in the cardamom, ground star anise, cinnamon, grated nutmeg, and salt; lastly, add the almond and vanilla extract and mix to combine well.
4. Add the chopped almonds to the batter and stir again. Next, pour the prepared batter into the greased muffin tin.
5. Add 1 cup of water and a metal rack to the bottom of your Instant Pot. Lower the muffin tin onto the rack.
6. Secure the lid. Choose the "Manual" mode and cook for 9 minutes under High pressure. Once cooking is complete, use a natural pressure release; carefully remove the lid.
7. Transfer your muffins to a cooling rack before unmolding and serving. Bon appétit!

4. Oatmeal with Blueberries and Honey

Servings 3

Ready in about
10 minutes

NUTRITIONAL INFORMATION
(Per serving)

405 - Calories
5.5g - Fat
78.2g - Carbs
13.4g - Protein
25.5g - Sugars
9g - Fiber

Ingredients

- 3 cups water
- 1 cinnamon stick
- 1 vanilla bean
- 1 ½ cups old-fashioned oats
- A pinch of sea salt
- A pinch of grated nutmeg (optional)
- 1/2 cup fresh blueberries
- 3 tablespoons honey

Directions

1. Place the water, cinnamon stick, vanilla bean, old-fashioned oats, salt, and nutmeg in the inner pot of your Instant Pot. Gently stir to combine.
2. Spoon the hot oatmeal into individual bowls; top with fresh blueberries; afterwards, drizzle 1 tablespoon of honey over each serving. Bon appétit!

5. Giant Greek Tiganites

Servings 6

**Ready in about
45 minutes**

**NUTRITIONAL
INFORMATION
(Per serving)**

320 - Calories
9g - Fat
48.2g - Carbs
10.3g - Protein
15g - Sugars
1.4g - Fiber

Ingredients

- A pinch of sea salt
- A pinch of granulated sugar
- 2 cups plain flour
- 1 teaspoon baking soda
- 1 teaspoon baking powder
- 1/2 teaspoon ground Mahleb
- 1/2 tablespoon orange rind, finely grated
- 1/4 teaspoon ground cloves
- 1 teaspoon vanilla extract
- 3 eggs, beaten
- 1 tablespoon coconut oil, melted
- 1 cup Greek yogurt
- 1 cup milk
- 1/4 cup warm honey
- 1/4 cup walnuts, chopped

Directions

1. Thoroughly combine the salt, sugar, flour, baking soda, baking powder, ground Mahleb, orange rind, ground cloves, and vanilla extract; mix until everything is well combined.
2. In another bowl, beat the eggs with the coconut oil, Greek yogurt, and milk. Add the egg mixture to the spiced flour mixture; stir until everything is well combined.
3. Then, spritz the bottom and sides of the inner pot with cooking spray.
4. Secure the lid. Choose the "Manual" mode and cook for 40 minutes under Low pressure. Once cooking is complete, use a quick pressure release; carefully remove the lid.
5. Cut your pancake into six wedges and drizzle warm honey over them. Scatter the chopped walnuts over the top and serve warm. Enjoy!

6. Old-Fashioned Sweet Bread

Servings 8

**Ready in about
50 minutes**

**NUTRITIONAL
INFORMATION
(Per serving)**

291 - Calories
14.1g - Fat
34.2g - Carbs
7.3g - Protein
13.3g - Sugars
1.4g - Fiber

Ingredients

- 1 cup oat flour
- 1 cup farina flour
- 1/2 teaspoon bicarbonate baking soda
- 1 cup caster sugar
- 1/2 teaspoon sea salt
- 1 ¼ cups Greek yogurt
- 1 egg, beaten
- 1 stick butter, melted
- 1/4 cup Sultanas, soaked for 15 minutes

Directions

1. In a mixing bowl, thoroughly combine the flour, baking soda, caster sugar, and salt. In a separate bowl, whisk the Greek yogurt, egg and melted butter.
2. After that, add the wet yogurt mixture to the dry mixture. Fold in the soaked Sultanas and gently stir until everything is well combined.
3. Add 4 cups of water and a metal trivet to the inner pot. Scrape the dough into a lightly greased heat-resistant container.
4. Cover with a piece of foil and lower it onto the metal trivet.
5. Secure the lid. Choose the "Cake" mode and cook for 40 minutes at High pressure. Once cooking is complete, use a natural pressure release for 5 minutes; carefully remove the lid.
6. Transfer your bread to a wire rack and let it rest before slicing and serving. Bon appétit!

7. Fruit and Quinoa Breakfast Casserole

Servings 6

Ready in about 20 minutes + chilling time

NUTRITIONAL INFORMATION (Per serving)

285 - Calories
3.7g - Fat
58.6g - Carbs
7.2g - Protein
32.7g - Sugars
4g - Fiber

Ingredients

- 1/2 cup honey
- 1/2 teaspoon ground cardamom
- 1/4 teaspoon ground anise
- 1/2 teaspoon rum extract
- A pinch of salt
- A pinch of grated nutmeg (optional)
- 1 ¼ cups quinoa
- 1/4 cup orange juice
- 1 cup coconut milk
- 2 ripe peaches, pitted, peeled and mashed
- 1 banana, mashed

Directions

1. Mix all of the ingredients in the order listed above. Cover and place in your refrigerator for at least 3 hours.
2. Next, preheat your oven to 360 degrees F and grease the sides and bottom of a baking dish with nonstick cooking oil. Scrape the fruit/quinoa batter into the prepared baking dish.
3. Add 1 cup of water and a metal rack to the bottom of the inner pot. Lower the baking dish onto the rack.
4. Secure the lid. Choose the "Steam" mode and cook for 10 minutes at High pressure. Once cooking is complete, use a quick pressure release; carefully remove the lid.
5. Afterwards, broil your casserole approximately 3 minutes and serve at room temperature. Bon appétit!

8. Omelet Mason Jars with Tuna

Servings 3

Ready in about 25 minutes

NUTRITIONAL INFORMATION (Per serving)

389 - Calories
26.8g - Fat
9g - Carbs
26.9g - Protein
5g - Sugars
1g - Fiber

Ingredients

- 2 tablespoons olive oil
- 1 purple onion, chopped
- 2 garlic cloves, minced
- 1/2 cup tomatoes, chopped
- 6 eggs, whisked
- 1/4 cup Greek yogurt
- 1/4 cup ricotta cheese, at room temperature
- 4 ounces tuna, chopped into pieces
- 4 tablespoons goat cheese, crumbled
- Sea salt and cayenne pepper, to taste
- 1/4 teaspoon ground bay leaf
- 1/2 teaspoon dried parsley flakes

Directions

1. Press the "Sauté" button to preheat your Instant Pot. Heat the oil until sizzling; now, sauté the onion until tender and translucent.
2. Add the garlic to the inner pot; let it cook an additional minute and immediately press the "Cancel" button.
3. Spritz the bottom and sides of 3 mason jars with cooking spray. Scrape the sautéed mixture into the jars. Add the chopped tomatoes to the jars.
4. Now, beat the eggs with the Greek yogurt and ricotta cheese. Fold in the tuna and goat cheese; sprinkle with salt, cayenne pepper, ground bay leaf, and parsley flakes. Slowly divide the egg/yogurt mixture between your jars.
5. Pour 1 cup of water into the inner pot. Place the trivet on top; place the mason jars on the trivet.
6. Secure the lid. Choose the "Manual" mode and cook for 15 minutes at High pressure. Once cooking is complete, use a natural pressure release; carefully remove the lid.
7. Carefully remove the mason jars from the Instant Pot. Serve warm.

9. Perfect Morning Porridge

Servings 5

Ready in about 20 minutes

NUTRITIONAL INFORMATION (Per serving)

349 - Calories
11.9g - Fat
46.2g - Carbs
14.5g - Protein
8.5g - Sugars
8.1g - Fiber

Ingredients

- 3 cups coconut milk
- 1 cup water
- 3 tablespoons chia seeds
- 1 cup quinoa, rinsed and drained
- 1/2 cup bulgur
- A pinch of grated nutmeg
- A pinch of sea salt
- 1/2 teaspoon ground cardamom
- 1/2 teaspoon ground anise
- 1/4 teaspoon ground cloves
- 1/2 cup black currants

Directions

1. Add all of the ingredients to the inner pot of your Instant Pot
2. Secure the lid. Choose the "Manual" mode and cook for 6 minutes at High pressure. Once cooking is complete, use a natural pressure release for 5 minutes; carefully remove the lid.
3. Serve with some extra honey if desired. Enjoy!

SOUPS & STEWS

10. Fava Bean Soup

Servings 5

**Ready in about
30 minutes**

NUTRITIONAL
INFORMATION
(Per serving)

133 - Calories
2.9g - Fat
19.7g - Carbs
11.5g - Protein
8.8g - Sugars
7.3g - Fiber

Ingredients

- 2 tablespoons olive
- 1 carrot, diced
- 1 parsnip, diced
- A bunch of scallions, chopped
- 5 cups roasted vegetable broth, preferably homemade
- 2 tablespoons tomato paste
- 1/4 teaspoon dried dill
- 1 teaspoon dried parsley flakes
- 1/4 teaspoon ground black pepper
- Sea salt, to taste
- 3/4 pound fava beans

Directions

1. Press the "Sauté" button to preheat your Instant Pot. Heat the oil and cook the carrot, parsnip, and scallions, stirring frequently, for 4 minutes or until they are just tender.
2. Now, stir in the other ingredients; gently stir to combine.
3. Secure the lid. Choose the "Soup/Broth" mode and cook for 20 minutes at High pressure. Once cooking is complete, use a quick pressure release; carefully remove the lid.
4. Serve hot.

11. Italian Red Lentil Soup

Servings 5

**Ready in about
15 minutes**

**NUTRITIONAL
INFORMATION
(Per Serving)**

330 - Calories
9.9g - Fat
43g - Carbs
21.2g - Protein
3.2g - Sugars
7.9g - Fiber

Ingredients

- 2 tablespoons olive oil
- 1 bell pepper, seeded and diced
- 1 pepperoncino, seeded and diced
- 1 carrot, diced
- 1 parsnip, diced
- 1/2 cup scallions, chopped
- 1 tablespoon Italian seasoning mix
- 1 ½ cups red lentils
- 2 vine-ripe tomatoes, crushed
- 1/4 teaspoon ground bay leaf
- 6 cups vegetable broth
- Sea salt and ground black pepper, to taste
- 1/2 cup taralli crackers

Directions

1. Press the "Sauté" button to preheat your Instant Pot. Then, heat the oil; once hot, sauté the peppers, carrot, parsnip, and scallions until they have softened and fragrant.
2. Then, add the Italian seasoning mix, lentils, tomatoes, bay leaf, ad vegetable broth. Bring to a boil and immediately press the "Cancel" button. Season with salt and pepper to taste.
3. Secure the lid. Choose the "Manual" mode and cook for 2 minutes at High pressure. Once cooking is complete, use a quick pressure release; carefully remove the lid.
4. Serve with traditional taralli crackers. Bon appétit!

12. Creamy Sopa de Zapallo

Servings 4

Ready in about
25 minutes

**NUTRITIONAL
INFORMATION**
(Per serving)

166 - Calories
4.6g - Fat
30.3g - Carbs
4.7g - Protein
4.3g - Sugars
.3g - Fiber

Ingredients

- 1 tablespoon ghee, melted
- 1/2 cup sweet onions, chopped
- 1/2 cup carrots, chopped
- 2 cloves garlic, peeled and minced
- 2 pounds summer squash, peeled and diced
- 1/4 teaspoon cumin
- Se salt, to taste
- 1/2 teaspoon ground white pepper
- 1 cup vegetable broth
- 1/2 cup almond milk, unsweetened

Directions

1. Press the "Sauté" button to preheat your Instant Pot. Then, melt the ghee; once hot, sauté the sweet onions and carrots until just tender.
2. Now, stir in the garlic and continue sautéing an additional 30 seconds.
3. Add the summer squash, cumin, salt, white pepper, and vegetable broth to the inner pot of your Instant Pot.
4. Secure the lid. Choose the "Manual" mode and cook for 15 minutes at High pressure. Once cooking is complete, use a quick pressure release; carefully remove the lid.
5. Then, transfer the mixture to your blender; pour in the almond milk. Process the mixture, working in batches, until it forms a creamy consistency.
6. Serve in individual bowls, garnished with queso fresco.

13. Classic Minestrone with a Twist

Servings 4

Ready in about 25 minutes

NUTRITIONAL INFORMATION (Per serving)

186 - Calories
5.6g - Fat
23.9g - Carbs
11.7g - Protein
5.8g - Sugars
4.5g - Fiber

Ingredients

- 1 tablespoon ghee, at room temperature
- 1 shallot, chopped
- 1 bell pepper, seeded and sliced
- 1 cup turnip, diced
- 1 cup potatoes, diced
- 1/2 cup zucchini, diced
- 1/2 teaspoon ginger-garlic paste
- 2 vine-ripe tomatoes, pureed
- 5 cups chicken broth
- 3/4 cup Cannellini beans, soaked overnight
- 1/2 teaspoon dried basil
- 1/2 teaspoon dried rosemary
- 1/2 teaspoon mixed peppercorns, freshly cracked
- 1/3 cup Acini di pepe
- 2 tablespoons balsamic vinegar
- 1 charred corn on the cob, kernels sliced off

Directions

1. Press the "Sauté" button to preheat your Instant Pot and melt the ghee. Cook the shallot until tender and translucent.
2. Next, add the peppers, turnip, potatoes and cook for a further 5 minutes, stirring periodically.
3. Stir the zucchini, ginger-garlic paste, tomatoes, chicken broth, beans, basil, rosemary, and peppercorns into the inner pot.
4. Secure the lid. Choose the "Manual" mode and cook for 12 minutes at High pressure. Once cooking is complete, use a quick pressure release; carefully remove the lid.
5. Next, stir in the Acini di pepe. Secure the lid. Choose the "Manual" mode and cook for 8 minutes under High pressure. Once cooking is complete, use a quick pressure release; carefully remove the lid.
6. Ladle the soup into individual bowls; drizzle balsamic vinegar over each serving. Scatter charred corn kernels over the top and serve hot!

14. Rich French Soup

Servings 4

**Ready in about
1 hour**

**NUTRITIONAL
INFORMATION
(Per serving)**

483 - Calories
30.1g - Fat
36.3g - Carbs
18.6g - Protein
18.1g - Sugars
3.5g - Fiber

Ingredients

- 2 tablespoons olive oil
- 3 cups Mayan sweet onions, thinly sliced
- 1 cup French shallots, thinly sliced
- 2 garlic cloves, minced
- 2 tablespoons dry sherry
- Sea salt and ground white pepper, to taste
- 1/4 teaspoon red chili flakes
- 1/2 teaspoon dried thyme
- 2 Turkish bay laurel leaves
- 5 cups chicken stock
- 1 cup heavy cream
- 4 diagonal slices of soft bread (avoid chewy artisan bread)
- 4 slices Gruyère cheese
- 4 slices Cheddar cheese

Directions

1. Press the "Sauté" button to preheat your Instant Pot and warm the oil; once hot, sauté the onion and leeks until they are tender and aromatic, approximately 11 minutes.
2. Adjust the "Sauté" function to less and let it cook an additional 20 minutes or until they are caramelized.
3. Next, stir in the garlic and let it cook an additional minute. Add a splash of dry sherry and let it simmer for 2 to 3 minutes or until mostly evaporated.
4. Add the salt, pepper, red chili flakes, thyme, Turkish bay laurel, and chicken stock.
5. Secure the lid. Choose the "Soup/Broth" mode and cook for 20 minutes at High pressure. Once cooking is complete, use a quick pressure release; carefully remove the lid.
6. Fold in the heavy cream and stir to combine well. Place the bread slices in a single layer on a cookie sheet. Bake in the preheated oven at 390 degrees F for 10 minutes, turning them over halfway through the cooking.
7. Ladle the soup into four ramekins; add the toasted bread and top with the cheese; broil in the preheated oven until the cheese bubbles. Enjoy!

15. Spicy Chunky Beef Soup

Servings 4

Ready in about 30 minutes

NUTRITIONAL INFORMATION (Per serving)

366 - Calories
18.3g - Fat
16.9g - Carbs
32.9g - Protein
5.7g - Sugars
2.5g - Fiber

Ingredients

- 1 tablespoon olive oil
- 1 pound lean ground beef
- 1/2 cup Spanish onions, sliced into rings
- 3 garlic cloves, chopped
- 1 turnip, diced
- 1 parsnip, diced
- 1 carrot, diced
- 1/2 teaspoon Spanish paprika
- Sea salt, to taste
- 1/2 teaspoon mixed peppercorns, preferably freshly cracked
- 1 Nora pepper, minced
- 2 cups water
- 2 cups cream of mushroom soup
- 2 ripe tomato, pureed
- 1/2 teaspoon fennel seeds
- 1/2 teaspoon basil
- 1 tablespoon fresh tarragon, chopped

Directions

1. Press the "Sauté" button to heat up your Instant Pot. Then, heat the oil until sizzling and sear the ground beef for 4 to 5 minutes, stirring with a wide spatula to ensure even cooking. Reserve.
2. Now, in the pan drippings, sauté the Spanish onions until tender. Fold in the chopped garlic and continue to sauté an additional 30 seconds.
3. Add the turnip, parsnip, and carrot to the inner pot. Season with the Spanish paprika, salt, and mixed peppercorns.
4. Stir the Nora pepper, water, cream of mushroom soup, pureed tomatoes, fennel seeds, and basil into the inner pot. Fold in the reserved meat.
5. Secure the lid. Choose the "Soup/Broth" mode and cook for 20 minutes at High pressure. Once cooking is complete, use a quick pressure release; carefully remove the lid.
6. Serve garnished with fresh tarragon. Enjoy!

16. Spanish Stew with Green Beans

Servings 4

Ready in about 25 minutes

NUTRITIONAL INFORMATION (Per serving)

179 - Calories
8.3g - Fat
24.3g - Carbs
5.5g - Protein
11.6g - Sugars
8.5g - Fiber

Ingredients

- 2 tablespoons olive oil
- 1 parsnip, thinly sliced
- 1 shallot, chopped
- 2 cloves garlic, chopped
- 2 bell peppers, seeded and sliced
- 1/4 cup red Spanish wine
- 1 zucchini, diced
- 1 eggplant, diced
- 2 ripe tomatoes, pureed
- 1 cup vegetable broth
- 1/2 teaspoon dried rosemary
- 1/2 teaspoon dried basil
- 1/3 teaspoon ground cumin
- 1/2 teaspoon Spanish paprika
- Sea salt and freshly cracked black pepper, to taste
- 1 cup green beans, fresh or thawed

Directions

1. Press the "Sauté" button to heat up your Instant Pot. Then, heat the oil until sizzling and cook the parsnip, shallot, garlic, and bell peppers until just tender and fragrant.
2. Add a splash of wine to deglaze the pan.
3. Then, add the zucchini, eggplant, tomatoes, the remaining wine, broth, rosemary, basil, cumin, Spanish paprika, salt, and black pepper to the inner pot.
4. Secure the lid. Choose the "Meat/Stew" mode and cook for 20 minutes at High pressure. Once cooking is complete, use a quick pressure release; carefully remove the lid.
5. After that, stir in the green beans; cover and let it sit in the residual heat until it wilts. Serve in soup bowls and enjoy!

17. Fisherman's Tilapia and Chickpea Stew

Servings 5

Ready in about 15 minutes

NUTRITIONAL INFORMATION (Per serving)

368 - Calories
11.5g - Fat
37.6g - Carbs
32.2g - Protein
7.6g - Sugars
8.5g - Fiber

Ingredients

- 2 tablespoons olive oil
- 1 teaspoon ginger-garlic paste
- 1 teaspoon thyme
- 1/2 teaspoon rosemary
- Sea salt and ground black pepper, to taste
- 1 teaspoon cayenne pepper
- 1 shallot, chopped
- 1 carrot, chopped
- 1 parsnip, chopped
- 1 celery rib, chopped
- 2 cups water
- 2 chicken bouillon cubes
- 1 pound tilapia, cut into bite-sized chunks
- 10 ounces can chickpeas, drained
- 2 vine-ripe tomatoes, pureed
- 1 ½ cups fresh okra
- 1 cup garlic crackers
- 2 tablespoons fresh cilantro leaves, chopped

Directions

1. Press the "Sauté" button to heat up your Instant Pot. Heat the oil and sauté the aromatics. Stir in the shallots, carrot, parsnip, and celery and continue to sauté an additional 2 to 3 minutes or until they are just tender.
2. Next, add the water, bouillon cubes, tilapia, chickpeas, tomatoes, and okra to the inner pot of your Instant Pot.
3. Secure the lid. Choose the "Manual" mode and cook for 5 minutes at High pressure. Once cooking is complete, use a quick pressure release; carefully remove the lid.
4. Ladle into individual bowls, garnish with garlic crackers and cilantro and serve hot.

MAIN DISHES

18. Crunchy Couscous Salad

Servings 4

**Ready in about
15 minutes**

**NUTRITIONAL
INFORMATION
(Per serving)**

325 - Calories
19.4g - Fat
25.6g - Carbs
12.2g - Protein
5.5g - Sugars
2.8g - Fiber

Ingredients

- 2 cups couscous
- 4 cups lettuce, torn into pieces
- 3 Roma tomatoes, sliced
- 1 Lebanese cucumber, sliced
- 1 carrot, julienned
- 2 tablespoons green olives, pitted and sliced
- 2 green garlic stalks, chopped
- 2 tablespoons olive oil
- 1/4 cup red wine vinegar
- Sea salt and freshly cracked black pepper, to taste
- 1 tablespoon fresh parsley, minced
- 1/2 pound feta cheese, crumbled

Directions

1. Add the couscous and 3 cups of water to the inner pot of your Instant Pot.
2. Secure the lid. Choose the "Manual" mode and cook for 5 minutes at High pressure. Once cooking is complete, use a quick pressure release; carefully remove the lid.
3. Drain and fluff your couscous with a fork. Add in the vegetables and gently stir to combine.
4. Drizzle olive oil and wine vinegar over your salad. Season with salt, black pepper, and parsley and toss again.
5. Top with crumbled feta cheese and serve well chilled. Enjoy!

19. Herby Juicy Chicken Fillets

Servings 4

**Ready in about
20 minutes**

**NUTRITIONAL
INFORMATION
(Per serving)**

357 - Calories
18.4g - Fat
0.6g - Carbs
43.2g - Protein
0.3g - Sugars
0g - Fiber

Ingredients

- 2 tablespoons olive oil
- 4 chicken fillets
- 1/4 cup red wine
- 3/4 cup chicken broth
- Sea salt and freshly ground black pepper, to taste
- 1/2 teaspoon dried marjoram
- 1 teaspoon dried sage
- 1/2 teaspoon dried parsley flakes
- 1/2 teaspoon dried basil

Directions

1. Press the "Sauté" button and adjust to the highest setting. Heat the oil and sear the chicken fillets for about 8 minutes, turning them over once or twice to ensure even cooking.
2. Pour in the red wine and scrape up the browned bits. Add the rest of the above ingredients.
3. Secure the lid. Choose the "Poultry" mode and cook for 5 minutes at High pressure. Once cooking is complete, use a natural pressure release; carefully remove the lid. Bon appétit!

20. Wild Rice Pilaf with Beans

Servings 4

Ready in about 30 minutes

NUTRITIONAL INFORMATION (Per Serving)

384 - Calories
5.6g - Fat
67g - Carbs
19.4g - Protein
5.2g - Sugars
9.6g - Fiber

Ingredients

- 1 tablespoon olive oil
- 1/2 cup shallots, chopped
- 1/2 cup artichoke hearts, chopped
- 2 garlic cloves, minced
- 1 ½ cups wild rice
- 1/2 cup red kidney beans
- 3 cups vegetable broth
- 1 chili pepper, minced
- 1 teaspoon sage
- 1 teaspoon thyme
- Sea salt and ground black pepper, to taste
- 2 ripe tomatoes, pureed

Directions

1. Press the "Sauté" button to preheat your Instant Pot. Then, sauté the shallots, artichoke and garlic for 2 to 3 minutes.
2. Add the remaining ingredients to the inner pot of your Instant Pot.
3. Secure the lid. Choose the "Manual" mode and cook for 20 minutes at High pressure. Once cooking is complete, use a quick pressure release; carefully remove the lid.
4. Ladle into individual bowls and serve warm. Bon appétit!

21. Ligurian Seafood Stew

Servings 3

**Ready in about
15 minutes**

**NUTRITIONAL
INFORMATION**
(Per serving)

353 - Calories
15.4g - Fat
20.8g - Carbs
34.7g - Protein
5.2g - Sugars
3.3g - Fiber

Ingredients

- 2 tablespoons olive oil
- 2 sweet Italian peppers, thinly sliced
- 1/2 cup purple onion, chopped
- 1 teaspoon fresh garlic, minced
- 1 chili pepper, minced
- 2 tomatoes, crushed
- 1/2 pound tuna, cut into bite-sized pieces
- 1/2 pound tiger prawns, deveined
- 1 teaspoon cayenne pepper
- 1 teaspoon fennel seeds
- Sea salt and freshly ground black pepper, to taste
- A pinch of dried chili flakes
- 1/2 cup dry white wine
- 1/2 cup clam broth
- 1/4 cup fresh basil leaves, snipped

Directions

1. Press the "Sauté" button to preheat your Instant Pot; heat the olive oil. Now, sauté the Italian peppers, purple onion, garlic, and chili pepper until just tender and fragrant.
2. Add a splash of wine to deglaze the pot. Add the remaining ingredients, except for the fresh basil, to the inner pot. Gently stir to combine.
3. Secure the lid. Choose the "Manual" mode and cook for 5 minutes at High pressure. Once cooking is complete, use a natural pressure release; carefully remove the lid.
4. Fill individual bowls with your stew, garnish with basil leaves and serve. Bon appétit!

22. Arroz con Pollo with a Twist

Servings 5

Ready in about 15 minutes

NUTRITIONAL INFORMATION (Per serving)

435 - Calories
19.4g - Fat
37.6g - Carbs
28.7g - Protein
2.8g - Sugars
5.6g - Fiber

Ingredients

- 2 tablespoons olive oil
- 1 Spanish onion, chopped
- 1 teaspoon garlic, minced
- 2 sweet peppers, diced
- 5 chicken drumsticks, boneless and chopped
- 2 cups water
- 1 cup cream of onion soup
- 2 Roma tomatoes, pureed
- 1 teaspoon Mojo Picante
- 1 teaspoon Spanish paprika
- 2 thyme sprigs, chopped
- 1 rosemary sprig, chopped
- Sea salt and ground black pepper, to taste
- 1 ½ cups orzo, rinsed

Directions

1. Press the "Sauté" button to preheat your Instant Pot; heat 1 tablespoon of olive oil until it just starts smoking. Sauté the Spanish onion, garlic, and sweet peppers until they are tender and fragrant; reserve.
2. Heat the remaining tablespoon of olive oil and adjust your Instant Pot to the highest setting. Sear the chicken until golden-brown and crispy.
3. Add in the water, cream of onion soup, tomatoes, Mojo Picante, Spanish paprika, thyme, rosemary, salt, and black pepper.
4. Lastly, stir in the orzo and bring to a rolling boil.
5. Secure the lid. Choose the "Manual" mode and cook for 6 minutes at High pressure. Once cooking is complete, use a natural pressure release; carefully remove the lid.
6. Taste, adjust the seasonings and serve warm.

23. Creamiest Seafood Chowder Ever

Servings 5

Ready in about 25 minutes

NUTRITIONAL INFORMATION (Per serving)

419 - Calories
12.6g - Fat
52.9g - Carbs
25.7g - Protein
7.9g - Sugars
8.4g - Fiber

Ingredients

- 1 tablespoon ghee, melted
- 1 bell pepper, seeded and chopped
- 1 carrot, chopped
- 1/2 cup leeks, chopped
- 1 parsnip, chopped
- 5 medium-sized potatoes, peeled and diced
- 1/2 teaspoon ground cumin
- 1/2 teaspoon ground coriander
- 1/2 teaspoon dried oregano
- 1 teaspoon garlic, pressed
- 5 cups water
- 3 vegetable bouillon cubes
- 1/2 pound codfish, cut into bite-sized chunks
- 1/2 pound shrimp, cleaned, deveined
- 1 cup double cream
- 2 teaspoons cornstarch
- 2 cups frozen green peas

Directions

1. Press the "Sauté" button to preheat your Instant Pot; melt the ghee. Once hot, sauté the bell pepper, carrot, leeks, parsnip, and potatoes until they are tender.
2. Now, stir in the ground cumin, coriander, oregano, and pressed garlic; stir an additional 30 seconds or so.
3. Now, add the water, vegetable bouillon cubes, fish, and shrimp to the inner pot.
4. Secure the lid. Choose the "Manual" mode and cook for 6 minutes at High pressure. Once cooking is complete, use a natural pressure release for 10 minutes; carefully remove the lid.
5. In a small mixing dish, whisk the cream with the cornstarch until well incorporated.
6. Fold the cream mixture into your chowder. Now, add in the green peas and press the "Sauté" button; press "Adjust" button and change the temperature to Less.
7. Let it simmer until the cooking liquid has reached the consistency you desire and green peas are heated through. Serve hot!

24. Shrimp Mélange with Bacon and Veggies

Servings 4

Ready in about 30 minutes

NUTRITIONAL INFORMATION (Per serving)

290 - Calories
6g - Fat
28.9g - Carbs
29.8g - Protein
5.5g - Sugars
6.2g - Fiber

Ingredients

- 2 ounces bacon
- 1 shallot, sliced
- 1 turnip, diced
- 2 carrots, sliced
- 4 cloves garlic, sliced
- 1/2 teaspoon Spanish paprika
- 1/2 teaspoon lemon thyme
- 1/2 teaspoon saffron
- 1 teaspoon fennel seeds
- 1/2 teaspoon mustard seeds
- Sea salt, to taste
- 4 cups beef bone broth
- 2 ripe tomatoes, puréed
- 1 tablespoon Worcestershire sauce
- 1 pound raw shrimp, cleaned and divined
- 1 tablespoon potato starch

Directions

1. Press the "Sauté" button to preheat your Instant Pot; then, sear the bacon until it releases easily from the pan; chop the bacon and reserve.
2. Now, in the pan drippings, sauté the shallot, turnip, and carrots until they have softened. Add in the garlic and seasonings; let them cook an additional 30 to 40 seconds or until they are aromatic.
3. Add the beef bone broth and tomatoes to the inner pot of your Instant Pot.
4. Secure the lid. Choose the "Manual" mode and cook for 10 minutes at High pressure. Once cooking is complete, use a natural pressure release for 5 minutes; carefully remove the lid.
5. After that, add in the Worcestershire sauce and shrimp.
6. Secure the lid. Choose the "Manual" mode and cook for 3 minutes at High pressure. Once cooking is complete, use a quick pressure release; carefully remove the lid.
7. Afterwards, stir in the potato starch and let it simmer on the "Sauté" function on Less until the liquid has thickened slightly. Bon appétit!

25. King Prawns in Tomato Curry Sauce

Servings 4

Ready in about 45 minutes

NUTRITIONAL INFORMATION (Per serving)

285 - Calories
14.6g - Fat
16.9g - Carbs
24.1g - Protein
3.5g - Sugars
2g - Fiber

Ingredients

- 1 pound king prawns, deveined
- 1 teaspoon curry paste
- 1/2 teaspoon ground coriander
- Sea salt and ground black pepper, to taste
- 1/2 teaspoon turmeric powder
- 1/2 teaspoon mustard seeds
- 1 teaspoon garlic powder
- 1 teaspoon red chili flakes
- 1/2 teaspoon Spanish paprika
- 1/4 cup white wine
- 1/3 cup coconut milk
- 1 tablespoon olive oil
- 1 fennel, chopped
- 1 sweet Italian pepper, minced
- 1/2 cup shallots, chopped
- 1 teaspoon ginger-garlic paste
- 2 Roma tomatoes, chopped
- 2 cups cream of mushroom soup
- 1 lemon, cut into wedges

Directions

1. In a large-sized ceramic bowl, place the king prawns along with the curry paste, coriander, salt, black pepper, turmeric, mustard seeds, garlic powder, chili flakes, Spanish paprika, wine, and milk; let it sit in your refrigerator for 30 minutes.
2. Press the "Sauté" button to preheat your Instant Pot; then, heat the olive oil until sizzling. Sauté the fennel, Italian pepper, shallot, and ginger-garlic paste for 3 to 4 minutes, stirring frequently.
3. Add in the tomatoes and cream of mushroom soup.
4. Secure the lid. Choose the "Manual" mode and cook for 6 minutes at High pressure. Once cooking is complete, use a quick pressure release; carefully remove the lid.
5. Place the king prawns in the inner pot, discarding the marinade. Cook your prawns on the "Sauté" function on Less until they are pink.
6. Serve with lemon wedges. Bon appétit!

26. Layered Fish and Egg Salad

Servings 5

**Ready in about
15 minutes
+ chilling time**

**NUTRITIONAL
INFORMATION
(Per serving)**

326 - Calories
24.2g - Fat
5.4g - Carbs
21.2g - Protein
3.3g - Sugars
1.4g - Fiber

Ingredients

- 3/4 pound sea bass fillets
- 2 cups broccoli florets
- 2 cups Romaine lettuce, torn into pieces
- 2 teaspoons fresh lemon juice
- 1/2 cup plain Greek yogurt
- 1/2 cup mayonnaise
- 1 tablespoon yellow mustard
- 2 Roma tomatoes, sliced
- 1 red bell pepper, sliced
- 1 green bell pepper, sliced
- 1 Lebanese cucumbers, sliced
- 1 shallot, thinly sliced
- 1/2 cup radishes, thinly sliced
- 2 green garlic stalks, minced
- 1/2 teaspoon dried oregano
- 1 teaspoon dried basil
- 1/4 teaspoon ground black pepper, or more to taste
- Sea salt, to taste
- 4 hard-boiled eggs, sliced

Directions

1. Place 1 cup of water and a metal trivet on the bottom of the inner pot. Place the sea bass fillets into a single layer in the steamer basket; arrange the broccoli florets on top.
2. Secure the lid. Choose the "Steam" mode and cook for 3 minutes at High pressure. Once cooking is complete, use a quick pressure release; carefully remove the lid.
3. Arrange equal portions of the Romaine lettuce leaves in one layer on five salad plates. Drizzle lemon juice over lettuce leaves.
4. In a mixing bowl, thoroughly combine the Greek yogurt, mayonnaise, and yellow mustard. Fold in all of the vegetables along with the steamed broccoli. Season with oregano, basil, black pepper, and salt. Stir until everything is well incorporated.
5. Chop the fish and place on a bed of lettuce. Spoon the vegetable mixture over the fish layer. Top with the hard-boiled eggs and serve well chilled.

27. Mediterranean Chicken Bowl with Pine Nuts

Servings 4

Ready in about 25 minutes

NUTRITIONAL INFORMATION (Per Serving)

328 - Calories
20.6g - Fat
11.1g - Carbs
24.7g - Protein
5.9g - Sugars
2.1g - Fiber

Ingredients

- 1 pound chicken legs, skinless and cut into pieces
- 3 tablespoons olive oil
- 2 tablespoons red wine vinegar
- 1 ounce watercress, tough stalks removed and chopped
- 1 bell pepper, deseeded and chopped
- 1 sweet onion, sliced
- 2 cloves garlic, minced
- 1 cucumber, sliced
- 2 cups gem lettuce, leaves separated
- Sea salt and ground black pepper, to taste
- 1 teaspoon Spanish paprika
- 1/2 teaspoon marjoram
- 1/2 teaspoon oregano
- 4 tablespoons pine nuts

Directions

1. Add 1 cup of water and metal rack to the inner pot of your Instant Pot. Lower the chicken legs onto the metal rack.
2. Secure the lid. Choose the "Steam" mode and cook for 15 minutes at High pressure. Once cooking is complete, use a quick pressure release; carefully remove the lid.
3. Slice the chicken meat into bite-sized pieces and discard the bones. Transfer the meat to a large serving bowl.
4. Press the "Sauté" button to preheat your Instant Pot; then, heat 1 tablespoon of olive oil until sizzling. Sauté the sweet onion and garlic until tender and fragrant or about 5 minutes. Add the remaining ingredients, except for the pine nuts, and stir to combine.
5. Add the mixture to the serving bowl and toss to combine well. Garnish with the pine nuts and serve immediately. Bon appétit!

28. Easy Fish Goulash

Servings 3

Ready in about 20 minutes

NUTRITIONAL INFORMATION (Per Serving)

261 - Calories
7.6g - Fat
24.9g - Carbs
26.1g - Protein
3.4g - Sugars
3.7g - Fiber

Ingredients

- 1 tablespoon olive oil
- 1 sweet Italian pepper, thinly sliced
- 1/2 cup shallots, chopped
- 1 parsnip, chopped
- 2 carrots, chopped
- 1/4 cup white wine
- 1 zucchini, sliced
- 2 garlic cloves, minced
- 3 cod fillets
- Sea salt and ground black pepper, to taste
- 1 teaspoon Creole seasoning
- 2 tomatoes, pureed
- 3 cups chicken bone broth
- 1 cup frozen sweet corn, thawed

Directions

1. Press the "Sauté" button to preheat your Instant Pot; then, heat 1 tablespoon of olive oil until sizzling. Sauté the Italian pepper, shallots, parsnip, and carrots for 3 to 4 minutes or until they have softened.
2. Add a splash of wine to deglaze the pan. Now, add in the zucchini, garlic, cod fillets, salt, black pepper, Creole seasoning, pureed tomatoes, and chicken bone broth.
3. Secure the lid. Choose the "Manual" mode and cook for 10 minutes at High pressure. Once cooking is complete, use a quick pressure release; carefully remove the lid.
4. After that, fold in the sweet corn. Cover with the lid and let it sit in the residual heat until it is thoroughly warmed. Serve in individual bowls and enjoy!

29. Italian-Style Eggplant and Chicken Casserole

Servings 5

Ready in about 25 minutes

NUTRITIONAL INFORMATION (Per Serving)

281 - Calories
15.6g - Fat
13.2g - Carbs
23.6g - Protein
5.9g - Sugars
3.9g - Fiber

Ingredients

- 2 tablespoons olive oil
- 1 bell pepper, seeded and sliced
- A bunch of scallions, sliced
- 1 teaspoon ginger-garlic paste
- 1 red chili pepper, minced
- 1 ¼ pounds ground chicken
- Sea salt, to taste
- 1/2 teaspoon cayenne pepper
- 1/4 teaspoon ground coriander
- 1/2 teaspoon rosemary, minced
- 2 vine-ripe tomatoes, pureed
- 1 pound eggplant, sliced
- 1/2 cup chicken bone broth
- 1 cup Pangrattato (Italian breadcrumbs)

Directions

1. Press the "Sauté" button to preheat your Instant Pot. Heat the olive oil and sauté the bell pepper and scallions until just tender and fragrant.
2. Stir in the ginger-garlic paste together with the red chili pepper; let it sauté an additional 30 seconds or until aromatic.
3. Fold in the ground chicken; continue to cook until it is golden brown. Add your spices and tomatoes; stir to combine well.
4. Place 1/2 of the eggplant slices on the bottom of a lightly greased baking dish. Add the meat mixture and top with the remaining eggplant slices. Pour in the chicken broth. Afterwards, scatter the Italian breadcrumbs on top.
5. Place 1 cup of water and metal trivet in the inner pot. Lower the baking dish onto the trivet.
6. Secure the lid. Choose the "Steam" mode and cook for 15 minutes at High pressure. Once cooking is complete, use a quick pressure release; carefully remove the lid.
7. You can broil this casserole if desired. Bon appétit!

30. Mackerel Fillets with Authentic Skordalia Sauce

Servings 3

Ready in about 15 minutes

NUTRITIONAL INFORMATION (Per Serving)

517 - Calories
33.6g - Fat
28g - Carbs
24.3g - Protein
2.4g - Sugars
3.6g - Fiber

Ingredients

- 3 mackerel fillets
- Sea salt and ground black pepper, to taste
- 1/2 teaspoon paprika
- 1 lemon, sliced
- Skordalia Sauce:
- 4 cloves garlic
- 1/2 teaspoon sea salt
- 2 mashed potatoes
- 4 tablespoons olive oil
- 2 tablespoons wine vinegar

Directions

1. Place 1/2 lemon and 1 cup of water in the inner pot. Place the rack on top. Arrange the mackerel fillets on the rack.
2. Sprinkle salt, black pepper, and paprika over the mackerel fillets.
3. Secure the lid. Choose the "Manual" mode and cook for 4 minutes at High pressure. Once cooking is complete, use a quick pressure release; carefully remove the lid.
4. Meanwhile, make the sauce by blending all of the ingredients in your food processor.
5. Garnish the mackerel fillets with the remaining lemon slices and serve with the Skordalia sauce on the side. Enjoy!

RICE

31. Sicilian-Style Brown Rice Salad

Servings 4

**Ready in about
20 minutes**

**NUTRITIONAL
INFORMATION
(Per Serving)**

457 - Calories
19.3g - Fat
62.3g - Carbs
10.4g - Protein
2.6g - Sugars
5.2g - Fiber

Ingredients

- 2 cups vegetable broth
- 1 ½ cups brown rice, rinsed
- 1/3 pound asparagus spears
- 1 purple onion, sliced
- 1/2 cup sun-dried tomatoes in oil, drained and chopped
- 1/4 cup ripe olives, pitted and halved

- Vinaigrette:
- 1/2 teaspoon fresh dill, minced
- 1/2 teaspoon fresh rosemary, minced
- Sea salt and ground black pepper, to taste
- 1 tablespoon yellow mustard
- 4 tablespoons olive oil
- 1/2 lemon, zested and juiced
- 1 teaspoon garlic, minced

Directions

1. Place the vegetable broth and brown rice in the inner pot of your Instant Pot.
2. Secure the lid. Choose the "Manual" mode and cook for 13 minutes at High pressure. Once cooking is complete, use a natural pressure release; carefully remove the lid.
3. Add the asparagus spears to the inner pot and seal the lid again. Choose the "Manual" mode and cook for 2 minutes at High pressure.
4. Once cooking is complete, use a quick pressure release; carefully remove the lid.
5. Transfer the cooked rice and asparagus to a serving bowl; add the purple onion, sun-dried tomatoes, and olives to the bowl and toss to combine.
6. Mix all ingredients for the vinaigrette; dress your salad and enjoy!

32. Traditional Yellow Rice

Servings 4

Ready in about 25 minutes

NUTRITIONAL INFORMATION (Per Serving)

158 - Calories
12.3g - Fat
15.7g - Carbs
0.4g - Protein
2.6g - Sugars
6.5g - Fiber

Ingredients

- Ground black pepper, to taste
- 1/2 teaspoon cayenne pepper
- 1/2 teaspoon celery seeds
- 1/2 teaspoon turmeric powder
- 1 bay laurel
- 1 cup vegetable broth
- 1 cup jasmine rice, rinsed
- 2 tablespoons ghee, melted

Directions

1. Add all of the above ingredients, except for the ghee, to the inner pot of your Instant Pot.
2. Secure the lid. Choose the "Manual" mode and cook for 9 minutes at High pressure. Once cooking is complete, use a natural pressure release for 10 minutes; carefully remove the lid.
3. Drizzle the melted ghee over each serving and enjoy!

33. Brown Rice with Vegetable and Pine Nuts

Servings 6

Ready in about
30 minutes

NUTRITIONAL
INFORMATION
(Per Serving)

288 - Calories
10.4g - Fat
43.5g - Carbs
7.4g - Protein
3.4g - Sugars
3.3g - Fiber

Ingredients

- 1 tablespoon olive oil
- 1/2 cup scallions, chopped
- 1 carrot, sliced
- 1 fennel, diced
- 1 pound zucchini, cut into thick sticks
- 1/2 teaspoon ground allspice
- 1 tablespoon ghee, at room temperature
- 1 ½ cups brown rice
- 6 cups water
- 1 teaspoon red pepper flakes
- Sea salt and ground black pepper, to taste
- 1/3 cup pine nuts, chopped

Directions

1. Press the "Sauté" button to preheat your Instant Pot. Heat the olive oil and sauté the scallions, carrot, and fennel until just tender and fragrant or about 4 minutes.
2. Add the zucchini and allspice; let it cook an additional 2 minutes or until thoroughly cooked; reserve.
3. After that, add the melted ghee to the inner pot; once hot, cook brown rice for 2 to 3 minutes. Add the water, red pepper, salt, and black pepper to the inner pot.
4. Secure the lid. Choose the "Manual" mode and cook for 20 minutes at High pressure. Once cooking is complete, use a quick pressure release; carefully remove the lid.
5. Fold in the sautéed mixture, cover with the lid, and let it sit in the residual heat until everything is thoroughly warmed. Garnish with pine nuts and serve warm. Enjoy!

34. Old-Fashioned Greek Rizogalo

Servings 4

Ready in about
25 minutes

NUTRITIONAL
INFORMATION
(Per Serving)

260 - Calories
2.2g - Fat
56.1g - Carbs
4.4g - Protein
17.2g - Sugars
1.4g - Fiber

Ingredients

- 1/4 teaspoon ground cardamom
- 1/8 teaspoon freshly grated nutmeg
- 1/2 teaspoon ground allspice berries
- 1/2 teaspoon ground cinnamon
- 1 teaspoon orange zest
- 1 cup white long-grain rice
- 1 ½ cups almond milk
- 2 tablespoons honey
- 4 tablespoons black currants
- 4 tablespoons almonds, slivered

Directions

1. Place the ground cardamom, nutmeg, allspice, cinnamon, orange zest, white rice, and almond milk in the inner pot of your Instant Pot.
2. Secure the lid. Choose the "Rice" mode and cook for 12 minutes at High pressure. Once cooking is complete, use a natural pressure release for 10 minutes; carefully remove the lid.
3. Spoon your rizogalo into individual bowls. Garnish with honey, black currants and almonds and serve warm.

35. Grandma's Chicken Pilau

Servings 4

Ready in about 30 minutes

NUTRITIONAL INFORMATION (Per Serving)

292 - Calories
16g - Fat
10.4g - Carbs
26.5g - Protein
4.8g - Sugars
2g - Fiber

Ingredients

- 1 tablespoon olive oil
- 4 chicken drumsticks, skinless and boneless
- 1/2 cup red onion chopped
- 1 red bell pepper, seeded and chopped
- 2 garlic cloves, pressed
- 1 teaspoon ginger, peeled and minced
- 1 cup chicken bone broth
- 3/4 cup brown rice
- 1/2 teaspoon ground allspice berries
- 1 cup tomato puree
- 1 teaspoon dried basil
- 1/2 teaspoon saffron
- 1/2 teaspoon dried parsley flakes
- 1/2 teaspoon fennel seeds
- Sea salt and ground black pepper, to season

Directions

1. Press the "Sauté" button to preheat your Instant Pot and heat the olive oil. Once hot, sear the chicken drumsticks for 2 to 3 minutes per side or until no longer pink. Reserve the chicken drumsticks, keeping them warm.
2. Then, cook the red onion and bell pepper in pan drippings until they have softened. After that, stir in the garlic and ginger and cook an additional minute or so.
3. Stir in the other ingredients along with the reserved chicken drumsticks.
4. Secure the lid. Choose the "Manual" mode and cook for 22 minutes at High pressure. Once cooking is complete, use a quick pressure release; carefully remove the lid.
5. The brown rice should not be mushy. Serve hot and enjoy!

36. Italian-Style Aromatic Risotto

Servings 5

Ready in about 25 minutes

NUTRITIONAL INFORMATION (Per Serving)

295 - Calories;
8.1g - Fat
44.1g - Carbs
10.8g - Protein
1.1g - Sugars
2g - Fiber

Ingredients

- 1 ½ cups Arborio rice
- 1/4 teaspoon ground bay laurel
- 1/4 teaspoon mustard seeds
- 1/2 teaspoon oregano
- 1/2 teaspoon basil
- 1/2 teaspoon thyme
- 2 cups roasted vegetable broth
- 1 cup Parmigiano-Reggiano cheese, preferably freshly grated

Directions

1. Place all ingredients, except for the Parmigiano-Reggiano cheese, in the inner pot of your Instant Pot.
2. Secure the lid. Choose the "Rice" mode and cook for 12 minutes at High pressure. Once cooking is complete, use a natural pressure release for 10 minutes; carefully remove the lid.
3. Ladle into serving bowls, garnish with cheese and serve immediately. Bon appétit!

37. Spanish Arroz Rojo with Beef

Servings 4

Ready in about 30 minutes

NUTRITIONAL INFORMATION (Per Serving)

520 - Calories
21.1g - Fat
46.2g - Carbs
35.9g - Protein
5.9g - Sugars
3.9g - Fiber

Ingredients

- 2 tablespoons olive oil
- 1 pound lean ground beef
- 1 Spanish onion, peeled and chopped
- 1 medium green pepper, deveined and chopped
- 1 Padrón pepper, deveined and minced
- 1/2 teaspoon fresh ginger, peeled and grated
- 2 garlic cloves, minced
- 2 tomatoes, pureed
- 2 tablespoons tomato paste
- 2 cups beef bone broth
- 1 teaspoon chili powder
- Coarse sea salt and ground black pepper, to taste
- 1 cup brown rice

Directions

1. Press the "Sauté" button to preheat your Instant Pot and heat 1 tablespoon of olive oil. Once hot, brown the ground beef for 3 to 4 minutes or until no longer pink; make sure to crumble with a fork and set aside.
2. Then, heat the remaining tablespoon of olive oil and sweat the Spanish onion for 2 to 3 minutes; add the peppers, ginger, and garlic and continue cooking an additional minute or until they are fragrant.
3. Add in the pureed tomatoes, tomato paste, beef bone broth, chili powder, salt, black pepper, and brown rice. Add the brown beef back to the inner pot.
4. Secure the lid. Choose the "Manual" mode and cook for 20 minutes at High pressure. Once cooking is complete, use a quick pressure release; carefully remove the lid. Enjoy!

38. Rice with Red Sauce and Graviera Cheese

Servings 4

Ready in about
15 minutes

NUTRITIONAL
INFORMATION
(Per Serving)

444 - Calories
15.1g - Fat
66g - Carbs
10.7g - Protein
5.3g - Sugars
3.9g - Fiber

Ingredients

- 1 ½ cups Basmati rice
- 2 cups water
- 1 cup grape tomatoes, halved
- 1/2 cup ripe olives, pitted and halved
- 2 roasted peppers, sliced into small pieces
- 2 tablespoons olive oil
- 1/2 cup spring onions, chopped
- Sea salt and red pepper flakes, to taste
- 1/2 teaspoon oregano
- 1/4 teaspoon garlic powder
- 4 ounces Graviera cheese
- 2 tablespoons fresh basil, snipped

Directions

1. Place the basmati rice and water in the inner pot of your Instant Pot.
2. Secure the lid. Choose the "Manual" mode and cook for 4 minutes at High pressure. Once cooking is complete, use a quick pressure release; carefully remove the lid.
3. Transfer the cooked rice to a serving bowl. Process the tomatoes, olives, red peppers, and olive oil in your blender until creamy and smooth.
4. Pour the tomato/pepper sauce over cooked rice. Add the spring onions, salt, pepper, oregano, and garlic powder; stir to combine.
5. Top with Graviera cheese and fresh basil. Serve immediately.

39. Mediterranean Spicy Jambalaya

Servings 4

Ready in about 20 minutes

NUTRITIONAL INFORMATION (Per Serving)

414 - Calories
6.8g - Fat;
63.7g - Carbs
24.2g - Protein
6.1g - Sugars
5.2g - Fiber

Ingredients

- 2 teaspoons olive oil
- 1/2 pound whole chicken, cut into bite-sized chunks
- 1 carrot, trimmed and chopped
- 1 shallot, chopped
- 2 sweet Italian peppers, deveined and chopped
- 1 red chili pepper, deveined and minced
- 2 cloves garlic, minced
- 1/2 teaspoon ground bay laurel
- 1 cup white rice
- 2 cups water
- Garlic salt and ground black pepper, to taste
- 1 tablespoon Old Bay seasoning
- 1/2 teaspoon file powder
- 2 chicken bouillon cubes
- 2 Roma tomatoes, pureed
- 2 tablespoons tomato paste
- 12 ounces frozen jumbo shrimp, peeled

Directions

1. Press the "Sauté" button to preheat your Instant Pot. Once hot, cook the chicken until it is no longer pink, stirring frequently; reserve.
2. Then, sweat the carrot, shallot, and peppers for 3 to 4 minutes, stirring continuously. Now, add the garlic and ground bay laurel to the inner pot; continue sautéing for a further 30 seconds.
3. Add the remaining ingredients to the inner pot of your Instant Pot; stir to combine. Stir in the reserved chicken.
4. Secure the lid. Choose the "Rice" mode and cook for 12 minutes at High pressure. Once cooking is complete, use a quick pressure release; carefully remove the lid. Bon appétit!

GRAINS, PASTA & BREADS

40. Couscous and Butternut Squash Bowl

Servings 4

**Ready in about
15 minutes**

**NUTRITIONAL
INFORMATION
(Per Serving)**

351 - Calories
4.6g - Fat
64.3g - Carbs
13.2g - Protein
0.8g - Sugars
5.3g - Fiber

Ingredients

- 1 tablespoon ghee, melted
- 1 pound butternut squash, peeled and sliced
- 1 carrot, sliced
- Sea salt and white pepper, to your liking
- 1/2 teaspoon Spanish paprika
- 1 ½ cups couscous
- 3 cups roasted vegetable broth, preferably homemade
- 1/4 teaspoon ground allspice berries
- 1/4 teaspoon ground cumin
- 2 tablespoons fresh Italian parsley leaves, chopped

Directions

1. Press the "Sauté" button to preheat your Instant Pot; heat olive oil. Once hot, cook the butternut squash and carrot until they are tender.
2. Stir in the sea salt, pepper, Spanish paprika, couscous, roasted vegetable broth, allspice, and cumin.
3. Secure the lid. Choose the "Manual" mode and cook for 6 minutes at High pressure. Once cooking is complete, use a quick pressure release; carefully remove the lid.
4. Garnish with fresh Italian parsley. Bon appétit!

41. Aromatic and Spicy Bulgur Wheat

Servings 5

Ready in about
25 minutes

NUTRITIONAL
INFORMATION
(Per Serving)

219 - Calories
6.3g - Fat
37.2g - Carbs
7.2g - Protein
1.3g - Sugars
5.6g - Fiber

Ingredients

- 2 tablespoons olive oil
- 1 red chili pepper, seeded and chopped
- 2 scallion stalks, chopped
- 1 teaspoon rosemary
- 1 teaspoon thyme
- 1 teaspoon fresh garlic, finely chopped
- 1 ½ cups bulgur wheat
- Sea salt and ground black pepper, to taste
- 1/4 teaspoon smoked paprika
- 2 vegetable bouillon cubes
- 2 cups water

Directions

1. Press the "Sauté" button to preheat your Instant Pot; heat olive oil. Once hot, cook the red chili pepper and scallions until they are tender.
2. Stir in the rosemary, thyme, and garlic; continue sautéing until they're aromatic.
3. After that, add the remaining ingredients to the inner pot and gently stir to combine.
4. Secure the lid. Choose the "Manual" mode and cook for 9 minutes at High pressure. Once cooking is complete, use a natural pressure release for 10 minutes; carefully remove the lid.
5. Serve immediately with your favorite Mediterranean cheese if desired. Enjoy!

42. Savory Mushroom Oatmeal

Servings 4

Ready in about 20 minutes

NUTRITIONAL INFORMATION
(Per Serving)

360 - Calories
12.7g - Fat
49g - Carbs
14.3g - Protein
1.3g - Sugars
7.4g - Fiber

Ingredients

- 1 tablespoon olive oil
- 2 cups button mushrooms, chopped
- 1 garlic clove, minced
- 2 scallion stalks, chopped
- 1 ½ cups rolled oats
- 2 cups water
- 1 ½ cups cream of mushroom soup
- 1/2 teaspoon turmeric powder
- 1/2 teaspoon cumin
- 1/4 teaspoon fennel seeds
- 1/4 teaspoon mustard seeds
- Coarse sea salt and ground black pepper, to taste

Directions

1. Press the "Sauté" button to preheat your Instant Pot. Heat the oil until sizzling. Now, sauté the mushrooms, garlic, and scallions until they have softened.
2. Add in the remaining ingredients; stir to combine.
3. Secure the lid. Choose the "Manual" mode and cook for 5 minutes at High pressure. Once cooking is complete, use a natural pressure release for 10 minutes; carefully remove the lid.
4. Spoon into individual bowls and serve warm. Bon appétit!

43. Spanish-Style Quinoa with Pinto Beans

Servings 3

Ready in about 20 minutes

NUTRITIONAL INFORMATION (Per Serving)

319 - Calories
8.8g - Fat
48.1g - Carbs
11.2g - Protein
6.3g - Sugars
9.3g - Fiber

Ingredients

- 2 tablespoons olive oil
- 2 bell peppers, seeded and chopped
- 1 teaspoon garlic, minced
- 1/2 cup shallots, chopped
- 1 ½ cups quinoa, rinsed
- 1 cup pinto beans, drained and rinsed
- 1 cup tomato sauce
- 1 cup vegetable broth
- 1 tablespoon Creole seasoning
- 1 teaspoon Spanish paprika
- 1 bay laurel
- Sea salt and ground black pepper, to taste
- 1/2 cup Kalamata olives, pitted and sliced

Directions

1. Press the "Sauté" button to preheat your Instant Pot. Heat the oil until sizzling. Now, sauté the bell peppers, garlic, and shallots until tender and fragrant.
2. Stir the quinoa, pinto beans, tomato sauce, broth, and spices into the inner pot of your Instant Pot.
3. Secure the lid. Choose the "Manual" mode and cook for 1 minute at High pressure. Once cooking is complete, use a natural pressure release for 5 minutes; carefully remove the lid.
4. Serve warm, garnished with Kalamata olives. Bon appétit!

44. Yellow Cornmeal with Mediterranean Ragout

Servings 3

**Ready in about
30 minutes**

**NUTRITIONAL
INFORMATION
(Per Serving)**

284 - Calories
7.2g - Fat
51.1g - Carbs
10.6g - Protein
13g - Sugars
10.3g - Fiber

Ingredients

- 3 cups water
- 3 bouillon cubes
- 3/4 cup whole-grain yellow cornmeal
- 1 tomato, pureed
- 1 tablespoon olive oil
- 1 medium-sized eggplant, diced
- 2 scallion stalks, chopped
- 6 ounces mushrooms, thinly sliced
- 1 red bell pepper, deveined and diced
- 1 teaspoon garlic, minced
- 1 teaspoon dried rosemary
- 1 teaspoon dried parsley flakes
- Sea salt and red pepper flakes, to your liking

Directions

1. Add the three cups of water, bouillon cubes, yellow cornmeal, and pureed tomato to the inner pot of your Instant Pot.
2. Secure the lid. Choose the "Manual" mode and cook for 9 minutes at Low pressure. Once cooking is complete, use a natural pressure release for 10 minutes; carefully remove the lid.
3. In the meantime, heat the olive oil in a nonstick skillet over moderate heat. Once hot, cook the vegetables for 5 to 6 minutes, until they have softened. Add in the aromatics and continue stirring for 30 seconds or so.
4. Taste and adjust the seasonings. Spoon the vegetable ragout over the hot cornmeal and serve right now. Enjoy!

45. Easy Herb Artisan Bread

Servings 10

**Ready in about
3 hours +
40 minutes**

**NUTRITIONAL
INFORMATION
(Per Serving)**

180 - Calories
3.3g - Fat
32.8g - Carbs
4.9g - Protein
0.3g - Sugars
2.2g - Fiber

Ingredients

- 2 ½ cups plain flour
- 1 cup whole-wheat flour
- 2 teaspoons sea salt
- 1/2 teaspoon brown sugar
- 1 teaspoon instant yeast granules
- 1 teaspoon fresh basil, chopped
- 1 teaspoon fresh rosemary, chopped
- 1/2 teaspoon marjoram
- 2 cups water, lukewarm
- 2 tablespoons olive oil

Directions

1. Thoroughly combine the flour, sea salt, brown sugar, instant yeast granules, and herbs. Pour in the water and stir until it is mixed thoroughly. The dough should be sticky.
2. Coat the bottom of the inner pot with a sheet of parchment paper; lower the dough ball onto the parchment paper.
3. Secure the lid. Choose the "Yogurt" mode on Low and let it proof for 3 hours. Knead the dough and set aside.
4. Brush your loaf with olive oil and transfer to a parchment-lined baking pan.
5. Bake in the preheated oven at 360 degrees F for 35 minutes. Your bread will be soft on the inside and crunchy on the outside. Bon appétit!

46. Banana Walnut Bread

(Ready in about 50 minutes | Servings 10)

Servings 10

Ready in about 30 minutes

NUTRITIONAL INFORMATION (Per Serving)

240 - Calories
10.6g - Fat
34.7g - Carbs
3.3g - Protein
17.2g - Sugars
1.5g - Fiber

Ingredients

- 1 ½ cups wheat flour
- A pinch of sea salt
- 3/4 teaspoon baking soda
- 4 tablespoons plain Greek yogurt
- 1 large egg
- 1/3 cup extra-virgin olive oil
- 1/2 cup good quality honey
- 1/2 teaspoon vanilla paste
- 1/4 teaspoon cardamom
- 1/4 teaspoon ground cloves
- 1/2 teaspoon cinnamon
- A pinch of grated nutmeg
- 2 ripe bananas, peeled and mashed
- 1/2 cup walnut hearts, chopped

Directions

1. In a mixing bowl, thoroughly combine the wheat flour with salt and baking soda.
2. In a separate mixing bowl, whisk the Greek yogurt, egg, olive oil, honey, and vanilla paste. Add your spices, banana, and walnut hearts to the batter.
3. Fold the wet yogurt mixture into the dry ingredients. Gently stir to combine.
4. Place 1 cup of water and a metal rack in the inner pot of your Instant Pot.
5. Secure the lid. Choose the "Manual" mode and cook for 45 minutes at High pressure. Once cooking is complete, use a quick pressure release; carefully remove the lid.
6. Transfer your banana bread to a wire rack to cool slightly before removing and slicing. Bon appétit!

47. Penne Pasta with Tomato Sauce and Mitzithra cheese

Servings 5

Ready in about
20 minutes

NUTRITIONAL INFORMATION
(Per Serving)

395 - Calories
15.6g - Fat
51.8g - Carbs
14.9g - Protein
2.5g - Sugars
7.5g - Fiber

Ingredients

- 2 tablespoons olive oil
- 2 scallion stalks, chopped
- 2 green garlic stalks, minced
- 10 ounces penne
- 1/3 teaspoon ground black pepper, to taste
- Sea salt, to taste
- 1/4 teaspoon cayenne pepper
- 1/4 teaspoon dried marjoram
- 1/2 teaspoon dried oregano
- 1/2 teaspoon dried basil
- 1/2 cup marinara sauce
- 2 cups vegetable broth
- 2 overripe tomatoes, pureed
- 1 cup Mitzithra cheese, grated

Directions

1. Press the "Sauté" button to preheat your Instant Pot. Heat the oil until sizzling. Now, sauté the scallions and garlic until just tender and fragrant.
2. Stir in the penne pasta, spices, marinara sauce, broth, and pureed tomatoes; do not stir, but your pasta should be covered with the liquid.
3. Secure the lid. Choose the "Manual" mode and cook for 7 minutes at High pressure. Once cooking is complete, use a natural pressure release for 5 minutes; carefully remove the lid.
4. Fold in the cheese and seal the lid. Let it sit in the residual heat until the cheese melts. Bon appétit!

48. All-Star Ziti Casserole

Servings 4

**Ready in about
25 minutes**

**NUTRITIONAL
INFORMATION
(Per Serving)**

552 - Calories
17.5g - Fat
80g - Carbs
16.2g - Protein
8.7g - Sugars
12.7g - Fiber

Ingredients

- 1 tablespoon olive oil
- 1 shallot, chopped
- 2 green garlic stalks, minced
- 2 bell peppers, chopped
- 1 teaspoon red chili pepper, minced
- 4 tablespoons cooking wine
- 2 overripe tomatoes, crushed
- 2 tablespoons coriander, minced
- 1/2 teaspoon basil
- 1/2 teaspoon sage
- 1/2 teaspoon thyme
- 1/2 teaspoon oregano
- 2 teaspoons kosher salt
- Salt and red cayenne pepper, to your liking
- 1 cup pasta sauce
- 1 cup condensed cream of mushroom soup
- 12 ounces ziti pasta
- 4 ounces feta cheese, crumbled
- 1/4 cup Graviera cheese, grated
- 1/2 cup dry breadcrumbs

Directions

1. Press the "Sauté" button to preheat your Instant Pot. Heat the oil until sizzling. Now, sauté the shallot, garlic, and peppers until just tender and fragrant.
2. Add a splash of the cooking wine to scrape up the dark spots from the bottom of the inner pot.
3. Add the tomatoes and bring it to a boil on "More" setting. Press the "Cancel" button. Stir in the spices, pasta sauce, condensed cream of mushroom soup, and ziti pasta.
4. Secure the lid. Choose the "Manual" mode and cook for 7 minutes at High pressure. Once cooking is complete, use a natural pressure release for 5 minutes; carefully remove the lid.
5. Transfer the mixture to an oven-safe casserole dish that is previously greased with cooking spray.
6. Top with the cheese and breadcrumbs. Bake in the preheated oven at 350 degrees F for 15 minutes or until it is bubbly. Let stand on a cooling rack for 10 minutes before slicing and serving. Enjoy!

BEANS & LEGUMES

49. Turkish Piyaz (Black Bean Salad)

Servings 3

Ready in about 30 minutes

NUTRITIONAL INFORMATION (Per Serving)

440 - Calories
21g - Fat
45.7g - Carbs
19.3g - Protein
6.7g - Sugars
12.7g - Fiber

Ingredients

- 3 cups water
- 2 bay laurels
- 1/2 pound dry borlotti beans
- 1 tablespoon lemon juice
- 1 tablespoon balsamic vinegar
- 4 tablespoons extra-virgin olive oil
- 1/2 teaspoon chili powder
- 1/4 teaspoon ground cumin
- Sea salt and red pepper flakes, to taste
- 1/2 cup cherry tomatoes, halved
- 1/2 cup red onion, thinly sliced
- 2 tablespoons fresh cilantro, chopped
- 1 sweet Italian pepper, seeded and thinly sliced
- 2 hard-boiled eggs, peeled and sliced
- 1/2 cup feta, crumbled

Directions

1. Place the water, bay laurels, and beans in the inner pot of your Instant Pot.
2. Secure the lid. Choose the "Bean/Chili" mode and cook for 25 minutes at High pressure. Once cooking is complete, use a quick pressure release; carefully remove the lid. Drain and let your beans cool completely.
3. Meanwhile, in a small bowl, whisk the lemon juice, balsamic vinegar, extra-virgin olive oil, chili powder, ground cumin, salt, and red pepper flakes; reserve the vinaigrette.
4. Transfer the chilled beans to a salad bowl. Add the cherry tomatoes, red onion, fresh cilantro, and Italian pepper.
5. Dress your salad and top with the hard-boiled eggs and feta cheese; serve well chilled. Bon appétit!

50. Chunky Chili con Carne

Servings 4

Ready in about 30 minutes

NUTRITIONAL INFORMATION (Per Serving)

581 - Calories
23.7g - Fat
53.3g - Carbs
41.2g - Protein
6.4g - Sugars
12.1g - Fiber

Ingredients

- 1 tablespoon olive oil
- 2 cloves garlic, minced
- 2 sweet Italian peppers, diced
- 2 green capsicums, minced
- 1/2 cup purple onion, chopped
- 1/2 pound ground turkey
- 1/2 pound ground sirloin
- 6 ounces ale beer
- 1 cup beef bone broth
- 1 teaspoon cocoa powder
- 8 ounces dry pinto beans, soaked overnight and drained
- 1 tablespoon Greek seasoning mix
- 1 cup pasta sauce
- 1 cup frozen sweet corn, thawed
- 1/4 cup feta cheese, cut into small cubes
- 1/2 cup black olives, pitted and halved

Directions

1. Press the "Sauté" button to preheat your Instant Pot. Heat the oil and sauté the garlic, peppers, onion, and ground meat until the onion is translucent and the ground meat is no longer pink.
2. Add a splash of ale to deglaze the bottom of the inner pot.
3. Now, add in the remaining ale, beef bone broth, cocoa powder, pinto beans, Greek seasoning mix, and pasta sauce.
4. Secure the lid. Choose the "Manual" mode and cook for 20 minutes at High pressure. Once cooking is complete, use a quick pressure release; carefully remove the lid.
5. Fold in the sweet corn and seal the lid. Let it stand in the residual heat until thoroughly warmed. Serve in individual bowls, garnished with feta cheese and black olives. Bon appétit!

51. Authentic Pasta e Fagioli

Servings 4

Ready in about 15 minutes

NUTRITIONAL INFORMATION (Per Serving)

486 - Calories
8.3g - Fat
95g - Carbs
12.4g - Protein
11.4g - Sugars;
14.8g - Fiber

Ingredients

- 2 tablespoons olive oil
- 1 teaspoon garlic, pressed
- 4 small-sized potatoes, peeled and diced
- 1 parsnip, chopped
- 1 carrot, chopped
- 1 celery rib, chopped
- 1 leek, chopped
- 1 (6-ounce) can tomato paste
- 4 cups water
- 2 vegetable bouillon cubes
- 8 ounces cannellini beans, soaked overnight
- 6 ounces elbow pasta
- 1/2 teaspoon oregano
- 1/2 teaspoon basil
- 1/2 teaspoon fennel seeds
- Sea salt, to taste
- 1/4 teaspoon freshly cracked black pepper
- 2 tablespoons Italian parsley, roughly chopped

Directions

1. Press the "Sauté" button to preheat your Instant Pot. Heat the oil and sauté the garlic, potatoes, parsnip, carrot, celery, and leek until they have softened.
2. Now, add in the tomato paste, water, bouillon cubes, cannellini beans, elbow pasta, oregano, basil, fennel seeds, freshly cracked black pepper, and sea salt.
3. Secure the lid. Choose the "Manual" mode and cook for 9 minutes at High pressure. Once cooking is complete, use a quick pressure release; carefully remove the lid.
4. Serve with fresh Italian parsley. Bon appétit!

52. Easiest Chickpea Salad Ever

Servings 4

Ready in about
20 minutes

NUTRITIONAL
INFORMATION
(Per Serving)

434 - Calories
18.1g - Fat
53.7g - Carbs
16.1g - Protein
12.2g - Sugars
10g - Fiber

Ingredients

- 1 thyme sprig
- 1 rosemary sprig
- 2 bay leaves
- 2/3 pound dried chickpeas, soaked
- 5 cups water

Salad:
- 1/4 cup balsamic vinegar
- 1/4 cup extra-virgin olive oil
- 1/2 cup radishes, sliced
- 1/2 cup cucumber, sliced
- 1 cup red cabbage, shredded
- 1 garlic clove, pressed
- 1 purple onion, thinly sliced
- Sea salt and crushed red pepper flakes, to your liking

Directions

1. Add the thyme sprig, rosemary, bay leaves, chickpeas, and water to the inner pot of your Instant Pot.
2. Secure the lid. Choose the "Manual" mode and cook for 13 minutes at High pressure. Once cooking is complete, use a natural pressure release for 5 minutes; carefully remove the lid.
3. Toss the slightly chilled chickpeas with the other ingredients; toss to combine well, taste and adjust the seasonings. Serve well chilled and enjoy!

53. Green Bean and Lentil Stew

Servings 5

Ready in about 20 minutes

NUTRITIONAL INFORMATION (Per Serving)

410 - Calories
7.7g - Fat
64.4g - Carbs
24.8g - Protein
8.3g - Sugars
12.2g - Fiber

Ingredients

- 2 tablespoons olive oil
- 1/2 cup celery stalks, chopped
- 1/2 cup parsnips, chopped
- 1 green bell pepper, seeds and chopped
- 1 red bell pepper, seeds and chopped
- 1 poblano pepper, seeds and finely chopped
- 1/2 cup leeks, chopped
- 1 teaspoon ginger-garlic paste
- 1/2 teaspoon dried basil
- 1/2 teaspoon dried oregano
- 1/2 teaspoon dried rosemary
- 1/2 teaspoon curry paste
- 2 cups brown lentils
- 3 cups vegetable broth
- 1/2 cup tomato paste
- Sea salt and freshly cracked black pepper, to taste
- 2 cups green beans, trimmed and halved

Directions

1. Press the "Sauté" button to preheat your Instant Pot. Heat the olive oil and sauté the celery, parsnip, peppers, and leeks until they are tender.
2. Stir in the aromatics, curry paste, lentils, broth, and tomato paste. Season with salt and pepper to taste.
3. Secure the lid. Choose the "Manual" mode and cook for 10 minutes at High pressure. Once cooking is complete, use a natural pressure release for 5 minutes; carefully remove the lid.
4. Add the green beans to the inner pot. Seal the lid, press the "Sauté" button, and adjust to "Less" temperature. Let it simmer until thoroughly heated. Bon appétit!

54. Traditional Greek Arakas Latheros

Servings 4

Ready in about 30 minutes

NUTRITIONAL INFORMATION (Per Serving)

358 - Calories
22.5g - Fat
29.4g - Carbs
11.2g - Protein
11.9g - Sugars
6.8g - Fiber

Ingredients

- 4 tablespoons Greek olive oil
- 1/2 cup shallots, chopped
- 1 red bell pepper, seeded and chopped
- 1/2 cup celery stalks and ribs, chopped
- 1 fennel, chopped
- 1 cup roasted vegetable broth, preferably homemade
- 2 tablespoons tomato paste
- 1 ½ cups overripe tomatoes, pureed
- 1 tablespoon Greek seasoning mix
- 1/4 teaspoon mustard seeds
- 1 bay laurel
- 1 ½ pounds sugar snap peas
- 4 thick slices bread, cubed
- 1/4 teaspoon coarse sea salt
- 2 tablespoons extra-virgin olive oil
- 1 teaspoon dried oregano

Directions

1. Press the "Sauté" button to preheat your Instant Pot. Heat the olive oil and sweat the shallots for 3 to 4 minutes. Then, add the bell pepper, celery, and fennel to the inner pot; continue cooking until they have softened.
2. Next, stir in the roasted vegetable broth, tomato paste, pureed tomatoes, Greek seasoning mix, mustard seeds, bay laurel, and sugar snap peas.
3. Secure the lid. Choose the "Manual" mode and cook for 18 minutes at High pressure. Once cooking is complete, use a quick pressure release; carefully remove the lid.
4. Meanwhile, crisp the bread cubes in a pan over moderate heat; fry your croutons with sea salt, olive oil, and dried oregano, stirring periodically.
5. Serve the warm peas with homemade croutons on the side.

55. Old-Fashion Snow Pea Chowder

Servings 4

Ready in about 25 minutes

NUTRITIONAL INFORMATION (Per Serving)

165 - Calories
5g - Fat
23.6g - Carbs
7.2g - Protein
11g - Sugars
6.5g - Fiber

Ingredients

- 1 tablespoon olive oil
- 1 red bell pepper, chopped
- 1 green bell pepper, chopped
- 2 carrots, trimmed and chopped
- 1 celery rib, chopped
- 1 cup leeks, chopped
- 2 garlic cloves, minced
- 3/4 pound snow peas
- 1 teaspoon cayenne pepper
- 1/4 teaspoon ground bay leaf
- 1/4 teaspoon ground cumin
- 1/4 teaspoon dried rosemary, crushed
- 1/2 teaspoon dried mint, crushed
- Sea salt and ground black pepper, to taste
- 1/2 cup plain Greek yogurt

Directions

1. Press the "Sauté" button to preheat your Instant Pot. Heat the olive oil and cook the peppers, carrot, celery, and leeks until they are tender and fragrant.
2. Stir in the garlic and continue sautéing for a further 30 seconds. Add the snow peas, cayenne pepper, bay leaf, cumin, rosemary, mint, salt, and black pepper.
3. Secure the lid. Choose the "Manual" mode and cook for 18 minutes at High pressure. Once cooking is complete, use a natural pressure release for 5 minutes; carefully remove the lid. Serve with Greek yogurt on the side. Enjoy!

56. Sloppy Lentils in Pita

Servings 4

Ready in about 25 minutes

NUTRITIONAL INFORMATION (Per Serving)

315 - Calories
6.2g - Fat
51.6g - Carbs
16.2g - Protein
3.9g - Sugars
8.5g - Fiber

Ingredients

- 4 tablespoons marinara sauce
- 2 vegetable bouillon cubes
- 1/4 teaspoon cumin
- 1/2 teaspoon mustard seeds
- 1/2 teaspoon red pepper flakes
- 2 cups water
- 1 cup red lentil
- 4 whole-wheat pita bread (flatbread)
- 2 tomatoes, sliced
- 1 Lebanese cucumber, sliced
- 2 tablespoons fresh parsley
- 2 cups fresh lettuce leaves
- 1 tablespoon yellow mustard
- 4 tablespoons Greek yogurt
- 1 teaspoon honey
- 1 tablespoon olive oil
- 1 teaspoon fresh garlic, pressed

Directions

1. Place the marinara sauce, bouillon cubes, cumin, mustard seeds, red pepper flakes, water and lentils in the inner pot of your Instant Pot.
2. Secure the lid. Choose the "Manual" mode and cook for 10 minutes at High pressure. Once cooking is complete, use a quick pressure release for 5 minutes; carefully remove the lid.
3. Divide the lentil mixture between pitas; top with the tomato, cucumber, parsley, and lettuce. In a small mixing bowl, whisk the yellow mustard, Greek yogurt, honey, olive oil, and fresh garlic.
4. Drizzle the sauce over the vegetables; wrap each pita in foil and serve immediately. Enjoy!

57. Barbunya Pilaki (Turkish Bean Stew)

Servings 6

Ready in about
35 minutes

NUTRITIONAL
INFORMATION
(Per Serving)

335 - Calories
5.6g - Fat
54.2g - Carbs
19.6g - Protein
5.1g - Sugars
14g - Fiber

Ingredients

- 2 tablespoons olive oil
- 1 bell pepper, sliced
- 1/2 cup leeks, chopped
- 1 parsnip, sliced
- 1 celery stalk, sliced
- 1 teaspoon fresh garlic, minced
- 1 pound white beans, soaked at least 6 hours
- 2 tablespoons red pepper paste
- 10 ounces canned tomatoes, crushed
- Sea salt and freshly ground black pepper, to taste
- 1 cup vegetable broth
- 1 dry bay laurel leaf

Directions

1. Press the "Sauté" button to preheat your Instant Pot. Heat the olive oil and sauté the pepper, leeks, parsnip, celery until they are tender and fragrant.
2. Stir in the minced garlic and continue sautéing for a further 30 seconds, stirring continuously.
3. Add in the beans, followed by the red pepper paste, tomatoes, salt, black pepper, vegetable broth, and bay laurel leaf.
4. Secure the lid. Choose the "Bean/Chili" mode and cook for 30 minutes at High pressure. Once cooking is complete, use a quick pressure release; carefully remove the lid. Serve over hot rice if desired. Enjoy!

VEGETABLE & SIDE DISHES

58. Ultimate Vegetable Pot

Servings 4

Ready in about 20 minutes

NUTRITIONAL INFORMATION (Per Serving)

173 - Calories
4.3g - Fat
32.8g - Carbs
7g - Protein
14.3g - Sugars
8.9g - Fiber

Ingredients

- 1 tablespoon olive oil
- 1 red onion, thinly sliced
- 1 ½ cups vegetable broth, preferably homemade
- 1 carrot, sliced
- 1 celery rib, sliced
- 2 cloves garlic, minced
- 1/4 teaspoon cumin
- 1 sweet pepper, seeded and sliced
- 1 red chili pepper, seeded and sliced
- 1/2 pound broccoli florets
- 1 small-sized head cabbage, cut into wedges
- 1 teaspoon smoked paprika
- Sea salt and ground black pepper, to taste
- 2 tablespoons fresh chives, roughly chopped

Directions

1. Press the "Sauté" button to preheat your Instant Pot; heat the olive oil. Once hot, sauté the red onion until it is caramelized or about 7 minutes; make sure to add a splash of broth for a few times to deglaze the pan.
2. Add in the garlic and continue sautéing for 30 seconds more or until it is aromatic.
3. After that, add the remaining ingredients, except for the chives; stir to combine.
4. Secure the lid. Choose the "Manual" mode and cook for 5 minutes at High pressure. Once cooking is complete, use a quick pressure release; carefully remove the lid. Ladle into serving bowls and garnish with the chives. Bon appétit!

59. Spanish Repollo Guisado

Servings 5

Ready in about 15 minutes

NUTRITIONAL INFORMATION (Per Serving)

191 - Calories
6.4g - Fat
29.8g - Carbs
5.1g - Protein
14.4g - Sugars
7.8g - Fiber

Ingredients

- 2 tablespoons olive oil
- 1 large-sized Spanish onion, chopped
- 2 garlic cloves, minced
- 1/2 teaspoon cumin seeds
- 1 cup tomato sauce
- 1 cup water
- 2 tablespoons vegetable bouillon granules
- 1 tablespoon white wine vinegar
- 1/4 teaspoon ground bay leaf
- 1 teaspoon Spanish paprika
- 1/4 teaspoon ground black pepper, to taste
- Sea salt, to taste
- 2 pounds purple cabbage, slice into wedges

Directions

1. Press the "Sauté" button to preheat your Instant Pot; heat the olive oil. Once hot, sauté the Spanish onion until it is tender and translucent.
2. Add in the garlic and cumin seeds; continue to sauté an additional minute, stirring frequently. Stir the remaining ingredients, minus the vinegar, into the inner pot of your Instant Pot.
3. Secure the lid. Choose the "Manual" mode and cook for 5 minutes at High pressure. Once cooking is complete, use a quick pressure release; carefully remove the lid.
4. Ladle into soup bowls; drizzle the white vinegar over the vegetables just before serving. Enjoy!

60. Spring Wax Beans with New Potatoes

Servings 3

Ready in about 20 minutes

NUTRITIONAL INFORMATION (Per Serving)

399 - Calories
5.6g - Fat
80g - Carbs
11.4g - Protein
15.8g - Sugars
13.5g - Fiber

Ingredients

- 1 tablespoon olive oil
- 2 scallion stalks, chopped
- 5 new potatoes, scrubbed and halved
- 1 sweet pepper, seeded and sliced
- 2 green garlic stalks, chopped
- 1/2 cup tomato sauce
- 2 tablespoons tomato paste
- 1/2 teaspoon brown sugar
- 1/2 cup roasted vegetable broth
- 1 pound wax beans, trimmed
- Sea salt and ground black pepper, to taste

Directions

1. Press the "Sauté" button to preheat your Instant Pot; heat the olive oil until sizzling. Now, sauté the scallions and new potatoes until just tender and fragrant.
2. Stir in the sweet pepper and green garlic and continue to sauté an additional 30 seconds.
3. Add in the tomato sauce, tomato paste, brown sugar, vegetable broth, and wax beans. Season with salt and black pepper.
4. Secure the lid. Choose the "Manual" mode and cook for 3 minutes at High pressure. Once cooking is complete, use a natural pressure release for 10 minutes; carefully remove the lid.
5. Taste, adjust seasonings and serve. Bon appétit!

61. Red Skin Potato Mash with Pine Nuts

Servings 4

Ready in about 15 minutes

NUTRITIONAL INFORMATION (Per Serving)

315 - Calories
15.6g - Fat
39.9g - Carbs
7.4g - Protein
4.5g - Sugars
4.8g - Fiber

Ingredients

- 2 cups water
- 2 pounds red baking potatoes, peeled and cut into wedges
- 1/2 teaspoon tarragon, chopped
- 1 teaspoon sweet paprika
- 1/2 teaspoon rosemary
- 1 teaspoon garlic salt
- 1/4 teaspoon black pepper, freshly ground
- 2 tablespoons extra-virgin olive oil
- 1/3 cup plain Greek yogurt
- 1/2 cup pine nuts, toasted

Directions

1. Place the water and potatoes in the inner pot of your Instant Pot.
2. Secure the lid. Choose the "Manual" mode and cook for 5 minutes at High pressure. Once cooking is complete, use a quick pressure release; carefully remove the lid.
3. Add the tarragon, sweet paprika, rosemary, garlic salt, black pepper, and olive oil to the inner pot; use a potato masher to puree the ingredients.
4. Fold in the Greek yogurt and stir with a wire whisk until everything is well combined.
5. Garnish with pine nuts and serve. Bon appétit!

62. Steamed Artichokes with Aïoli Sauce

Servings 4

Ready in about 15 minutes

NUTRITIONAL INFORMATION (Per Serving)

266 - Calories
20.8g - Fat
18g - Carbs
5.6g - Protein
1.9g - Sugars
8.8g - Fiber

Ingredients

- 1/2 lemon, sliced
- 1 thyme sprig
- 1 rosemary sprig
- 4 medium-sized artichokes, cleaned
- Aïoli Sauce:
- 1/2 cup mayonnaise
- 1 teaspoon garlic, minced
- 2 teaspoon lemon juice, freshly squeezed
- Sea salt and ground black pepper, to taste

Directions

1. Throw the lemon, thyme, rosemary and 1 cup of water into the inner pot; add the steamer basket to the inner pot, too.
2. Arrange the artichokes in the basket.
3. Secure the lid. Choose the "Steam" mode and cook for 10 minutes at High pressure. Once cooking is complete, use a quick pressure release; carefully remove the lid.
4. Meanwhile, whisk all ingredients for the Aïoli sauce until well combined. Place the sauce in your refrigerator until ready to use.
5. Serve warm the artichokes with the chilled Aïoli on the side. Enjoy!

63. Creamy Parmesan Vegetables

Servings 4

Ready in about 15 minutes

NUTRITIONAL INFORMATION (Per Serving)

130 - Calories
4.5g - Fat
17.1g - Carbs
7.7g - Protein
6g - Sugars
4.5g - Fiber

Ingredients

- 2 bay laurels
- 1/2 pound carrot, sliced
- 1/2 pound broccoli florets
- 1/2 pound cauliflower florets
- Sea salt and cayenne pepper, to taste
- 1 teaspoon yellow mustard
- 2 ounces plain milk
- 1 tablespoon flour
- 1/2 cup parmesan cheese, grated

Directions

1. Place 2 bay laurels and 1 cup of water and a steamer basket in the inner pot of your Instant Pot. Throw the vegetables into the steamer basket.
2. Secure the lid. Choose the "Steam" mode and cook for 3 minutes at High pressure. Once cooking is complete, use a quick pressure release; carefully remove the lid.
3. Season your vegetables with salt and cayenne pepper.
4. Add the mustard, plain milk, flour, and parmesan cheese to the inner pot of your Instant Pot. Press the "Sauté" button on "Less" mode and let it simmer until heated through. Bon appétit!

64. Italian Cabbage with Portobello Mushrooms

Servings 4

Ready in about 15 minutes

NUTRITIONAL INFORMATION (Per Serving)

231 - Calories
8.1g - Fat
31.7g - Carbs
10.4g - Protein
16.7g - Sugars
8.9g - Fiber

Ingredients

- 2 tablespoons olive oil
- 1 Spanish onion, chopped
- 1 ½ pounds Portobello mushrooms, sliced
- 1 teaspoon garlic, minced
- 1/2 teaspoon tarragon
- 1/2 teaspoon basil
- 1/2 teaspoon thyme
- Sea salt and ground black pepper, to taste
- 1/2 teaspoon sweet paprika
- 1 pound green cabbage, cut into wedges
- 1 cup tomato sauce
- 1 cup vegetable broth

Directions

1. Press the "Sauté" button to preheat your Instant Pot; heat the olive oil until sizzling. Now, sauté the Spanish onion until tender and translucent.
2. Add in the Portobello mushrooms and garlic; let it sauté an additional minute, stirring continuously.
3. Throw the other ingredients into the inner pot of your Instant Pot.
4. Secure the lid. Choose the "Manual" mode and cook for 4 minutes at High pressure. Once cooking is complete, use a quick pressure release; carefully remove the lid.
5. Ladle into serving bowls and serve garnished with garlic croutons if desired. Bon appétit!

65. Mom's Brussels Sprouts with Herbs

Servings 5

Ready in about 15 minutes

NUTRITIONAL INFORMATION (Per Serving)

154 - Calories
8.3g - Fat
18.7g - Carbs
5.8g - Protein
5.3g - Sugars
6.3g - Fiber

Ingredients

- 2 tablespoons olive oil
- 1 bay laurel
- 1/2 teaspoon cumin seeds
- 1/4 teaspoon fennel seeds
- 1 tablespoon ghee, room temperature
- 1 sweet Italian pepper sliced
- 1 Spanish chili pepper, sliced
- 1 shallot, chopped
- 1 ½ pounds whole Brussels sprouts, trimmed
- 1 teaspoon ginger-garlic paste
- 1/4 cup tomato paste
- 1 cup vegetable broth, preferably homemade
- 1/2 teaspoon saffron
- Ground black pepper and Himalayan salt, to taste

Directions

1. Press the "Sauté" button to preheat your Instant Pot; heat the olive oil until sizzling. Now, sauté the bay laurel, cumin, and fennel seeds until they are fragrant.
2. Then, melt the ghee on the "Sauté" function on "Normal" mode. Stir in the Italian pepper, Spanish chili pepper, and shallot and continue sautéing for a further 3 to 4 minutes.
3. After that, throw in the Brussels sprouts, ginger-garlic paste, tomato paste, broth, saffron, black pepper, and Himalayan salt.
4. Secure the lid. Choose the "Manual" mode and cook for 4 minutes at High pressure. Once cooking is complete, use a quick pressure release; carefully remove the lid. Bon appétit!

66. Corn on the Cob with Feta and Herbs

Servings 5

Ready in about 15 minutes

NUTRITIONAL INFORMATION (Per Serving)

172 - Calories
5g - Fat
29.7g - Carbs
7.1g - Protein
5.6g - Sugars
4.2g - Fiber

Ingredients

- 5 ears corn
- 1/2 cup feta cheese, crumbled
- Coarse sea salt, to taste
- 1 teaspoon dried oregano
- 1/2 teaspoon dried basil
- 1/2 teaspoon dried rosemary

Directions

1. Remove the husks from your ears of corn. Place 1 cup of water and a metal trivet in the inner pot of your Instant Pot.
2. Now, transfer the husked corn to the trivet.
3. Secure the lid. Choose the "Manual" mode and cook for 4 minutes at High pressure. Once cooking is complete, use a quick pressure release; carefully remove the lid.
4. Top with the cheese, salt, oregano, basil, and rosemary and serve immediately. Bon appétit!

DESSERTS

67. Festive Orange Cheesecake

Servings 10

Ready in about 50 minutes + chilling time

NUTRITIONAL INFORMATION (Per Serving)

300 - Calories
18.7g - Fat
27.7g - Carbs
5.6g - Protein
11.9g - Sugars
0.5g - Fiber

Ingredients

Crust:
- 4 tablespoons butter, melted
- 1 ½ cups wafer cookies, crumbled
- 1 tablespoon fresh orange juice

Filling:
- 8 ounces plain full-fat Greek yogurt
- 10 ounces cream cheese
- 2/3 cup granulated sugar
- 1/2 teaspoon rum extract
- 1 teaspoon vanilla extract
- 1/4 teaspoon ground cinnamon
- A pinch of salt
- A pinch of grated nutmeg
- 1 tablespoon orange peel, grated
- 1 large-sized egg, at room temperature

Topping:
- 1/4 cup water
- 8 tablespoons frozen orange juice concentrate, thawed
- 1/4 cup sugar
- 1/2 tablespoon cornstarch

Directions

1. Cut out a round shape of parchment paper and place it at the bottom of a baking pan.
2. In a small bowl, combine the ingredients for the crust. Press the crust mixture evenly in the bottom of the prepared pan. Let it chill in your freezer for 20 minutes.
3. Meanwhile, beat the Greek yogurt and cream cheese until fluffy; stir in the sugar, spices, grated orange peel, and egg; blend well. Pour the mixture into the crust-lined pan.
4. Add 1 cup of water and metal rack to the bottom of the inner pot. Then, lower the baking pan onto the rack.
5. Secure the lid. Choose the "Manual" mode and cook for 22 minutes at High pressure. Once cooking is complete, use a natural pressure release for 5 minutes; carefully remove the lid.
6. In a small-sized saucepan, whisk all the topping ingredients until well combined. Cook until it is bubbly and thickened. Spoon the slightly cooled topping over your cheesecake.
7. Place in your refrigerator for 3 to 5 hours. Serve well chilled.

68. Mixed Berry and Peach Compote

Servings 5

Ready in about 20 minutes

NUTRITIONAL INFORMATION
(Per Serving)

167 - Calories
1.7g - Fat
28.6g - Carbs
1.7g - Protein
36.5g - Sugars
1.2g - Fiber

Ingredients

- 3 cups water
- 1/2 cup fresh pomegranate juice
- 1/2 cup granulated sugar
- 1 cinnamon stick
- 1 teaspoon cloves
- 1 vanilla bean
- 1 pound peaches, pitted and quartered
- 1/2 pound frozen mixed berries

Directions

1. Place all of the above ingredients in the inner pot of your Instant Pot.
2. Secure the lid. Choose the "Manual" mode and cook for 2 minutes at High pressure. Once cooking is complete, use a natural pressure release for 10 minutes; carefully remove the lid.
3. Serve with wafers and Greek yogurt if desired. Enjoy!

69. Easy Blueberry Crumb Cake

Servings 8

Ready in about 40 minutes

NUTRITIONAL INFORMATION (Per Serving)

322 - Calories
20g - Fat
33.1g - Carbs
4.2g - Protein
18.4g - Sugars
2.4g - Fiber

Ingredients

- 1 cup plain flour
- 1/2 teaspoon baking powder
- 1/4 teaspoon sea salt
- 1 ½ cups white sugar
- 1 cup milk
- 1/2 teaspoon vanilla paste
- 1 stick butter, at room temperature
- 2 cups fresh blueberries
- 1 tablespoon cornstarch

Directions

1. In a mixing bowl, thoroughly combine the flour, baking powder, salt, and 1 cup of sugar; slowly, pour in the milk and mix to combine.
2. Next, stir in the vanilla and butter; mix to combine.
3. Place 1 cup of water and metal rack in the inner pot of your Instant Pot. Brush a baking pan with 1 teaspoon of melted butter.
4. Arrange the fresh blueberries on the bottom of the baking pan; sprinkle with the remaining 1/2 cup of sugar and cornstarch.
5. Pour the batter over the fruit layer. Place the pan onto the rack.
6. Secure the lid. Choose the "Manual" mode and cook for 35 minutes at High pressure. Once cooking is complete, use a quick pressure release; carefully remove the lid.
7. A tester inserted into the center of your cake should come out dry and clean. Transfer to a cooling rack before slicing and serving. Bon appétit!

70. Apricot and Almond Crumble

Servings 6

Ready in about
30 minutes

NUTRITIONAL
INFORMATION
(Per Serving)

282 - Calories
11.5g - Fat
47.5g - Carbs
4.7g - Protein
28g - Sugars
4g - Fiber

Ingredients

- 1/3 cup almonds, chopped
- 1 cup rolled oats
- 1/2 cup plain flour
- 1/4 teaspoon ground cinnamon
- A pinch of grated nutmeg
- A pinch of salt
- 2 tablespoons honey
- 1/2 cup granulated sugar
- 1/3 cup ghee, room temperature
- 1/2 cup white sugar
- 2 teaspoons orange juice
- 10 apricots, pitted and quartered
- 1/2 teaspoon almond extract
- 1/2 teaspoon vanilla essence
- 1 ½ tablespoons arrowroot powder

Directions

1. In a mixing bowl, thoroughly combine the almonds, rolled oats, plain flour, cinnamon, nutmeg, salt, honey, 1/2 cup of granulated sugar, and ghee.
2. Scrape the batter into a parchment-lined baking pan.
3. Then, mix the apricots with the white sugar, orange juice, vanilla, almond extract, and arrowroot powder. Spoon the mixture into the baking pan.
4. Secure the lid. Choose the "Manual" mode and cook for 5 minutes at High pressure. Once cooking is complete, use a natural pressure release for 15 minutes; carefully remove the lid.
5. If you prefer a crispier topping, place your crumble under a preheated broiler for 2 to 3 minutes or until the top browns a little. Serve with vanilla ice cream if desired. Bon appétit!

71. Decadent Croissant Bread Pudding

Servings 6

Ready in about 20 minutes

NUTRITIONAL INFORMATION (Per Serving)

513 - Calories
27.9g - Fat
50.3g - Carbs
12.5g - Protein
25.7g - Sugars
3.8g - Fiber

Ingredients

- 1/2 cup double cream
- 6 tablespoons honey
- 1/4 cup rum, divided
- 2 eggs, whisked
- 1 teaspoon cinnamon
- A pinch of salt
- A pinch of grated nutmeg
- 1 teaspoon vanilla essence
- 8 croissants, torn into pieces
- 1 cup pistachios, toasted and chopped

Directions

1. Spritz a baking pan with cooking spray and set it aside.
2. In a mixing bowl, whisk the eggs, double cream, honey, rum, cinnamon, salt, nutmeg, and vanilla; whisk until everything is well incorporated.
3. Place the croissants in the prepared baking dish. Pour the custard over your croissants. Fold in the pistachios and press with a wide spatula.
4. Add 1 cup of water and metal rack to the inner pot of your Instant Pot. Lower the baking dish onto the rack.
5. Secure the lid. Choose the "Manual" mode and cook for 12 minutes at High pressure. Once cooking is complete, use a quick pressure release; carefully remove the lid.
6. Serve at room temperature or cold. Bon appétit!

72. Poached Apples with Greek Yogurt and Granola

Servings 4

Ready in about 15 minutes

NUTRITIONAL INFORMATION
(Per Serving)

247 - Calories
3.1g - Fat
52.6g - Carbs
3.5g - Protein
40g - Sugars
5.3g - Fiber

Ingredients

- 4 medium-sized apples, peeled
- 1/2 cup brown sugar
- 1 vanilla bean
- 1 cinnamon stick
- 1/2 cup cranberry juice
- 1 cup water
- 1/2 cup 2% Greek yogurt
- 1/2 cup granola

Directions

1. Add the apples, brown sugar, water, cranberry juice, vanilla bean, and cinnamon stick to the inner pot of your Instant Pot.
2. Secure the lid. Choose the "Manual" mode and cook for 5 minutes at High pressure. Once cooking is complete, use a natural pressure release for 5 minutes; carefully remove the lid. Reserve poached apples.
3. Press the "Sauté" button and let the sauce simmer on "Less" mode until it has thickened.
4. Place the apples in serving bowls. Add the syrup and top each apple with granola and Greek yogurt. Enjoy!

73. Jasmine Rice Pudding with Cranberries

Servings 4

**Ready in about
15 minutes**

**NUTRITIONAL
INFORMATION
(Per Serving)**

402 - Calories
3.6g - Fat
81.1g - Carbs
8.9g - Protein
22.3g - Sugars
2.2g - Fiber

Ingredients

- 1 cup apple juice
- 1 heaping tablespoon honey
- 1/3 cup granulated sugar
- 1 ½ cups jasmine rice
- 1 cup water
- 1/4 teaspoon ground cinnamon
- 1/4 teaspoon ground cloves
- 1/3 teaspoon ground cardamom
- 1 teaspoon vanilla extract
- 3 eggs, well-beaten
- 1/2 cup cranberries

Directions

1. Thoroughly combine the apple juice, honey, sugar, jasmine rice, water, and spices in the inner pot of your Instant Pot.
2. Secure the lid. Choose the "Manual" mode and cook for 4 minutes at High pressure. Once cooking is complete, use a natural pressure release for 5 minutes; carefully remove the lid.
3. Press the "Sauté" button and fold in the eggs. Cook on "Less" mode until heated through.
4. Ladle into individual bowls and top with dried cranberries. Enjoy!

74. Brandy Chocolate Fudge with Almonds

Servings 6

Ready in about 50 minutes

NUTRITIONAL INFORMATION (Per Serving)

255 - Calories
13.6g - Fat
30.9g - Carbs
7.7g - Protein
14.1g - Sugars
5.2g - Fiber

Ingredients

- 2 medium-sized eggs
- 2 tablespoons brandy
- 1 teaspoon vanilla extract
- A pinch of grated nutmeg
- A pinch of salt
- 1/2 cup ghee, room temperature
- 2/3 cup granulated sugar
- 1/4 teaspoon ground cloves
- 1/4 teaspoon ground cinnamon
- 1/2 cup cocoa powder
- 4 tablespoons almond meal
- 1/2 cup plain flour
- 1/2 teaspoon baking powder
- 1/2 cup dark chocolate, chopped into chunks
- 1/2 cup almonds, chopped

Directions

1. Beat the eggs until frothy; add in the brandy, vanilla, nutmeg, and salt; mix to combine. Add melted ghee and granulated sugar; whisk again to combine.
2. Stir in the ground cloves, cinnamon, cocoa powder, almond meal, and plain flour. After that, add the baking powder, chocolate, and almonds. Stir to combine and scrape the batter into a parchment-lined baking pan.
3. Add 1 cup of water and metal trivet to the inner pot. Lower the baking pan onto the trivet.
4. Secure the lid. Choose the "Manual" mode and cook for 30 minutes at High pressure. Once cooking is complete, use a natural pressure release for 15 minutes; carefully remove the lid.
5. Transfer your fudge to a wire rack before slicing and serving. Bon appétit!

75. Orange and Almond Cupcakes

Servings 9

Ready in about 20 minutes

NUTRITIONAL INFORMATION (Per Serving)

392 - Calories
18.7g - Fat
50.1g - Carbs
5.9g - Protein
25.2g - Sugars
0.7g - Fiber

Ingredients

Cupcakes:
- 1 orange extract
- 2 tablespoons olive oil
- 2 tablespoons ghee, at room temperature
- 3 eggs, beaten
- 2 ounces Greek yogurt

- 2 cups cake flour
- A pinch of salt
- 1 tablespoon grated orange rind
- 1/2 cup brown sugar
- 1/2 cup almonds, chopped

Cream Cheese Frosting:
- 2 ounces cream cheese
- 1 tablespoon whipping cream
- 1/2 cup butter, at room temperature

- 1 ½ cups confectioners' sugar, sifted
- 1/3 teaspoon vanilla
- A pinch of salt

Directions

1. Mix the orange extract, olive oil, ghee, eggs, and Greek yogurt until well combined.
2. Thoroughly combine the cake flour, salt, orange rind, and brown sugar in a separate mixing bowl. Add the egg/yogurt mixture to the flour mixture. Stir in the chopped almonds and mix again.
3. Place parchment baking liners on the bottom of a muffin tin. Pour the batter into the muffin tin.
4. Place 1 cup of water and metal trivet in the inner pot of your Instant Pot. Lower the prepared muffin tin onto the trivet.
5. Secure the lid. Choose the "Manual" mode and cook for 11 minutes at High pressure. Once cooking is complete, use a quick pressure release; carefully remove the lid. Transfer to wire racks.
6. Meanwhile, make the frosting by mixing all ingredients until creamy. Frost your cupcakes and enjoy!

53191546R00064